First Human Body Encyclopedia

DK | Penguin Random House

REVISED EDITION
Assistant editor Debangana Banerjee
Assistant art editor Kartik Gera
Art editor Shreya Sadhan
Project editor Suneha Dutta
Senior editor Shatarupa Chaudhuri
DTP designer Bimlesh Tiwary
CTS manager Balwant Singh
Managing editors Laura Gilbert,
Alka Thakur Hazarika
Managing art editors Diane Peyton Jones,
Romi Chakraborty
Senior producer, pre-production Ben Marcus
Producer Nicole Landau
Publisher Sarah Larter
Publishing director Sophie Mitchell
Jacket editor Ishani Nandi
Jacket designer Shreya Sadhan
Art director Stuart Jackman
Consultant Jack Challoner

ORIGINAL EDITION
Editors Ben Morgan, Zahavit Shalev
Design assistance Amy McSimpson
Additional design Jacqueline Gooden, Tory Gordon-Harris,
Claire Patane, Laura Roberts
Senior editor Penny Smith
Senior art editor Cheryl Telfer
DTP designer Almudena Díaz
Production controller Shivani Pandey
Managing art editor Clare Shedden
Publishing manager Sue Leonard
Illustrator Peter Bull
Digital illustrator Pilar Morales
Picture researchers Marie Ortu, Rob Nunn
Consultants Dr Penny Preston, Dr Frances Williams

First published in Great Britain in 2005
This edition first published in Great Britain in 2016 by
Dorling Kindersley Limited
80 Strand, London, WC2R 0RL

Copyright © 2005, © 2016
Dorling Kindersley Limited, London
A Penguin Random House Company

2 4 6 8 10 9 7 5 3 1
001–280451–Oct/2016

ISBN 978-0-24118-877-4

Printed and bound in Hong Kong

A WORLD OF IDEAS:
SEE ALL THERE IS TO KNOW

www.dk.com

Contents

Human body

Skeleton and bones

Moving muscles

Brain and senses

Heart and blood

Test yourself with the questions at the bottom of each page...

Circles show close-up images you might not otherwise be able to see.

Visual lists contain facts about related topics, such as taste.

Hands on activities show you how you can try things out for yourself.

About this book
This book has special features that will show you how to get your hands on as much information as possible! Use the "Turn and learn" buttons to find out more about a subject on other pages.

Your amazing body

The greatest machine you'll ever own is your body. It's more complicated than any computer, it lasts for a lifetime, and it's yours for free.

Turn and learn
Skeleton:
pp. 12-13
Digestion:
pp. 82-83

Body parts
Your body is made up of hundreds of different parts. You probably know the names of the bits you can see, but there are many more hidden deep inside you.

Hair

Forehead

Ears

Eyebrows

Cheeks

Nose

Eyes

Lips

Teeth

Inside your body
Doctors can see inside your body with special cameras. X-ray cameras take pictures of hard body parts like bones. Other cameras, called scanners, can see soft body parts.

Hands

Fingers

Wrists

Two of everything
Body parts often come in pairs. You have two feet, two eyes, two ears, two lungs, and so on. This means you have a handy spare in case one of them gets damaged.

A chest X-ray shows the bones in your chest. The white shape in the middle is the heart.

What do we call the study of the human body?

Water, water

Water is the most important chemical in your body. About two-thirds of your weight is water.

Picture detective

Take a look at the first few pages and see if you can find these pictures.

Robot

No substitute

The human body is too complicated for robots to copy. Robots can copy the way we walk, but they can't think or feel like we do.

The ingredients

Your body is made of just a few simple chemicals, apart from water.

 Carbon is the chemical in diamonds and coal. A fifth of you is carbon.

 Iron makes your blood red. You have enough to make one small iron nail.

 Phosphorus is in the tips of matches, as well as your bones and teeth.

 Sodium and **chlorine** make salt. Blood is one-third as salty as sea water.

 Potassium is used in some types of soap. It's also in your body fluids.

 Nitrogen is important in muscles. It's also the main ingredient in air.

Chimpanzee

Chimps have hands like ours.

Compared to chimps, our bodies look almost hairless.

Being human

Although we look different to animals, our bodies are similar on the inside. Our closest animal relatives are chimpanzees.

What makes you you?

All human bodies work the same way, but everyone is different. Nobody looks, sounds, or thinks exactly like you. You're different because of the way your genes and experience shape you as you grow up.

Uniqu
The shape of your face, th
colour of your hair, and man
other things make yo
unique – different fro
everyone else

Light brown eyes

Fair skin

Curly hair

Black hair

Freckles

6

In the genes

Genes are instructions that build your body and tell it how to work. Your genes control many of the things that make you unique, like the colour of your eyes or how tall you'll be.

This girl has genes that allow her to roll up her tongue. The boy doesn't have those genes, so he can't roll his tongue.

There's enough DNA inside you to stretch to the Sun and back 400 times.

DNA

Your genes are stored in a chemical called DNA, which looks like a twisted ladder with four different types of rung. The rungs make up a four-letter alphabet that spells out your genes, like letters in a book.

DNA can split and copy itself.

hands on

Look in a mirror and see if you can roll your tongue. Don't cheat by squeezing it with your lips. Test your family to see who has the gene.

Learning to ride a bike changes your brain and your body.

Changing body

Genes don't control everything – experience also shapes you. If you exercise a lot, for instance, your body gets stronger.

In the family

Your genes came from your parents. Half come from your mother and half come from your father. If you look like your parents, it's because you share the same genes.

About 20,000.

Building blocks

Every part of your body is made of tiny building blocks called cells, which fit together like bricks in a wall. Cells are so small that hundreds could fit on the point of a pin.

The nucleus controls the rest of the cell.

The inside of a cell is packed with a kind of living jelly called cytoplasm.

DNA is stored in the cell nucleus.

DNA

The skin on your fingertips is made of lots of small ridges.

Inside a cell

In the middle of a cell is its control centre – the nucleus. The nucleus sends instructions to the rest of the cell, telling the cell what chemicals to make.

The outer skin, or membrane, stops things from leaking out.

Tiny generators provide cells with power.

Before a cell divides, the nucleus splits to make two nuclei.

Making new cells

A cell makes new cells by dividing. The two new cells are half the size, but they soon grow back. Millions of your cells die every second, but millions of others divide to replace them.

The new cells pull apart and separate, but they usually stay close neighbours.

8

How big are cells?

Cells are too small to see with the naked eye, but scientists can photograph them through powerful microscopes. The cells on your skin are about a hundredth of a millimetre wide.

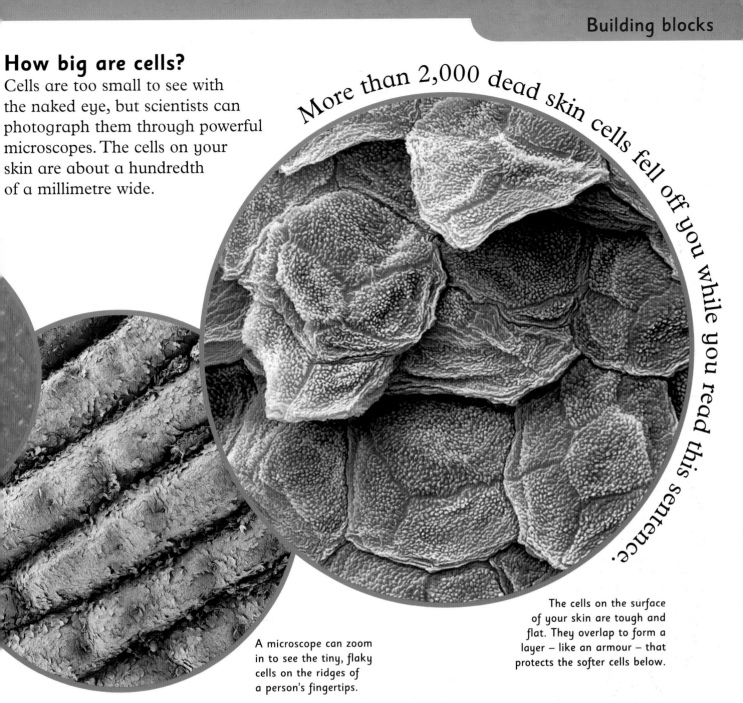

More than 2,000 dead skin cells fell off you while you read this sentence.

A microscope can zoom in to see the tiny, flaky cells on the ridges of a person's fingertips.

The cells on the surface of your skin are tough and flat. They overlap to form a layer – like an armour – that protects the softer cells below.

Fat cells are bubble-shaped. They store fat under your skin.

Many blood cells are red. They carry oxygen around the body.

Nerve cells are thin and wiry. They carry electrical signals.

Bone cells make your bones hard. They live in tiny holes in bones.

Cells make tissue

Your body contains about 200 different types of cells that do different jobs. Cells of the same type usually group together to form tissue. Fat, muscle, bone, and nerves are types of tissue. Blood is a liquid tissue.

Organizing the body

Your cells and tissues are organized into larger body parts called organs. In turn, your organs work together to form body systems.

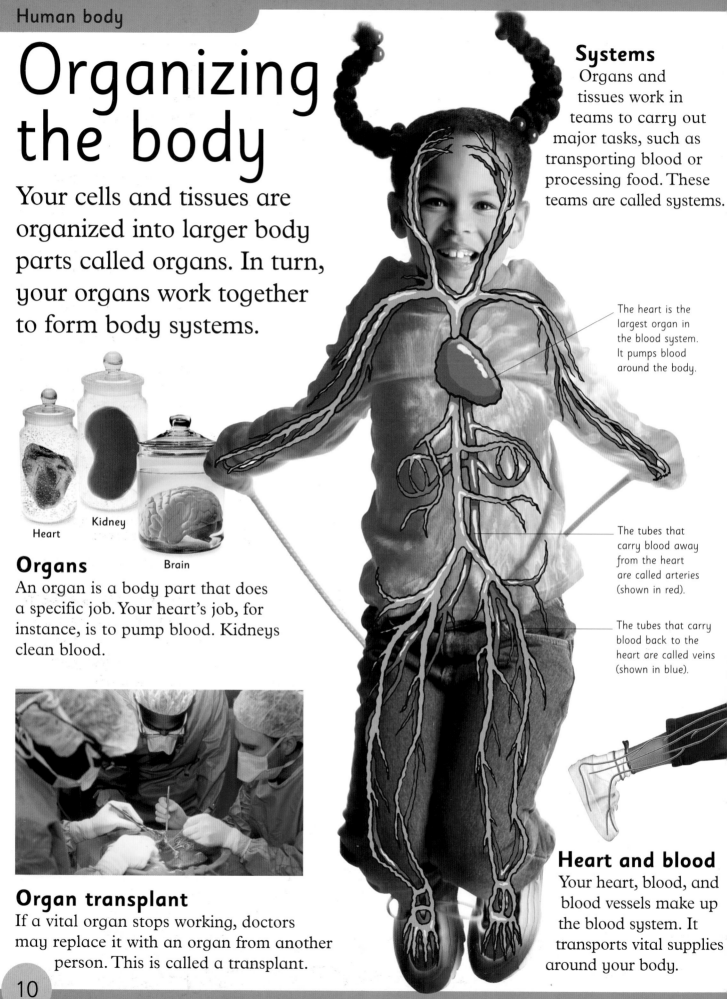

Systems
Organs and tissues work in teams to carry out major tasks, such as transporting blood or processing food. These teams are called systems.

The heart is the largest organ in the blood system. It pumps blood around the body.

Organs
An organ is a body part that does a specific job. Your heart's job, for instance, is to pump blood. Kidneys clean blood.

Heart

Kidney

Brain

The tubes that carry blood away from the heart are called arteries (shown in red).

The tubes that carry blood back to the heart are called veins (shown in blue).

Organ transplant
If a vital organ stops working, doctors may replace it with an organ from another person. This is called a transplant.

Heart and blood
Your heart, blood, and blood vessels make up the blood system. It transports vital supplies around your body.

Which body system makes your stomach rumble?

Muscles

Your muscle system is made of tissues that move parts of your body by pulling on them or squeezing them. Your biggest muscles all pull on bones.

our fingers are moved by muscles your arm.

Muscles change the position of your skeleton by pulling different bones.

The most powerful muscles are in your legs.

Other systems

Some of your other important systems are shown in this list.

In the **breathing system**, the main organs are your lungs, which take in air.

The **hormone system** uses powerful chemicals to control your body and mood.

Skin, hair, and nails, form your body's protective covering.

The **immune system** seeks and destroys germs that get into your body.

The **urinary system** cleans blood and gets rid of waste chemicals.

The **reproductive system** are the organs that make babies.

Skeleton

Bones and joints make up the skeletal system, an inner frame that supports the body.

A quarter of your bones are in your feet.

Digestive system

Your digestive organs break down food to provide your body with energy and raw materials.

Your mouth is the first part of the digestive system.

A long, twisting tube makes up your intestines, where digested food is absorbed.

Nerves

Your nervous system carries electrical signals around your body. You need this system to see, hear, think, and react.

Signals shoot along nerves to muscles, telling them when to pull.

Senses, such as touch, rely on nerve cells that send signals to your brain.

Your brain is the nervous system's control centre.

The digestive system.

11

Skeleton

Your bones all join up to make a frame for your body called the skeleton. This protects your insides, and helps you move about.

Smallest bone

One of the smallest bones in your body lies deep inside your ear. It is around the same length as a grain of rice.

A giraffe's long neck helps it to eat leaves off tall trees.

Neck bones

Did you know that you have seven bones in your neck, the same number as a giraffe? The top one allows you to move your head up and down, the second lets you rotate it

Skull

Jaw bone

Rib

The spine is made up of small bones called vertebrae.

Shoulder blade

Each finger has three bones, except for your thumb, which has two.

206 bones

There are 206 bones in an adult skeleton. Over half of these are found in the hands and feet – the parts of your body that perform the most complicated movements.

You have eight small bones in each wrist.

How many ribs have you got?

Frogs have very short spines to withstand the strain of the huge leaps they take.

A fish's spine allows it to bend its body from side to side so it can swim smoothly.

Snakes are incredibly bendy thanks to many identical vertebrae forming their long spines.

Other skeletons

Most animals have a backbone and are called vertebrates. Animals with no spine, such as spiders and bugs, are called invertebrates.

Your tail bone is at the very bottom of your spine.

Thigh bone

Shin bone

Your ankle has seven bones – three larger than the others.

There are 54 bones in your hands, and 52 in your feet.

The thigh bone is the biggest and strongest in the body.

Long lasting

Bone is a very hard material and one of the last parts to rot away when a body is buried. This woman lived in the Stone Age, 5,000 years ago, but her bones have survived until today.

Turn and learn

Bone and cartilage: **pp. 20–21**
Teeth: **pp. 84–85**

Head case

The most complex part of the skeleton is the skull. It is made of many bones that fit together tightly. The skull protects the brain and supports the face.

The frontal bone forms your forehead.

The cranium is the domed part of your skull

Helmet
The upper part of the skull is like a helmet that protects the brain. The lower part forms a structure for your facial features to attach to.

Eye sockets are made up of seven different bones.

The brain fills most of the cranium.

The front of the nose has no bones.

Facial features
This image shows the relationship between your skull and face. There are no bones shaping the front part of your nose, your lips, or your ears. Your nose and ears are shaped by cartilage.

Teeth are set into the upper and lower jaws.

14

There are two parts to the upper jaw.

The lower jaw is hinged. It is the only skull bone that can move.

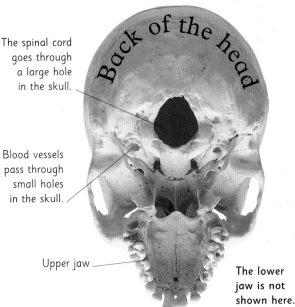

Back of the head

The spinal cord goes through a large hole in the skull.

Blood vessels pass through small holes in the skull.

Upper jaw

The lower jaw is not shown here.

Jigsaw

The skull bones fit together like the pieces of a jigsaw. All but one of the bones are locked in place. This makes the skull very strong.

Hole in the head

From underneath, you can clearly see the big hole at the bottom of this skull. The spinal cord – which runs down your back – meets your brain here.

Face from the past

Scientists can work out what a dead person's face looked like from their skull alone. They examine the facial bones and build up artificial cartilage, muscle, and skin over them.

Meet the relatives

Chimpanzees and humans share a common ancestor. However, chimps have smaller brains than humans, so their craniums are smaller. Chimps also have a large ridge above their eyes, and a jutting jaw.

15

Bendy backbone

Your spine is a length of bones running down your back. Without it, you couldn't hold up your head and body, or make any sort of movement.

The first seven bones are in your neck. They are known as the cervical vertebrae.

The next 12 are called the thoracic vertebrae.

Stack of bones
Your spine contains 24 separate bones called vertebrae. At the bottom are nine more vertebrae. They are much smaller and are fused together.

The thoracic vertebrae form joints with the ribs.

A straight back is actually quite curvy.

Your spine curves gently, a bit like the letter "s".

The five lumbar vertebrae bear most of your weight.

Back of spine

Front of spine

The fused bones of the sacrum and coccyx don't allow much movement.

The five sacral vertebrae are fused together.

The spinal cord goes through this hole.

The coccyx consists of four fused vertebrae.

Segments of the spine
Each vertebra has a strong, stubby section that supports the weight of your body, and a hole for the spinal cord to pass through.

16

What is a slipped disc?

Shock absorbers

You twist and bend your spine almost every time you move. Sandwiched between the vertebrae are pads of cartilage to stop them from banging and rubbing against each other and getting worn out.

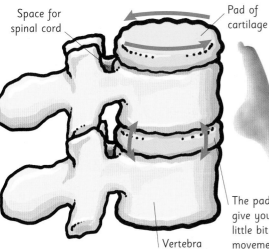

Space for spinal cord

Pad of cartilage

The pads give you a little bit of movement in all directions.

Vertebra

Ribcage

Your thoracic vertebrae connect to your ribs. Together, they form a cage around your heart and lungs. Rib bones are curved. They are also thinner and more bendy than the bones in your spine.

The shape of a woman's pelvis is different from a man's. This allows a baby to pass through it when she gives birth.

Pelvis

Reproductive organs and some digestive organs rest in the bowl-shaped hollow of your pelvis. The sacral vertebrae and coccyx form the bottom of the bowl.

You could be this bendy...

The way the back curves means we can't bend as far back as we can forwards.

Bendy backbone

The amount of movement between each vertebra and its neighbours is actually very small, but added together they allow for a large range of movement.

hands on

Bend over. Gently feel the bones of your spine with your fingertips. Can you follow them from neck to waist?

...with a lot of practice!

It's when one of the pads between the vertebrae gets damaged.

Living bone

Their outer surface may be hard and dry but that doesn't mean your bones aren't alive. Bones are always growing and repairing themselves.

Marrow can be found in the spine, skull, and the main leg and arm bones.

What's inside our bones?
Bone accounts for one sixth of your body's weight. Bones are built in such a way that it is often lighter than it looks.

Spongy bone
Parts of some bones have a honeycomb structure with lots of spaces. This makes them weigh lesser than if they were solid right through.

Bone marrow
A jelly-like substance called marrow fills the centre of many of your larger bones. It supplies your body with red blood cells at a rate of 3 million cells per second.

Compact bone
The hardest and most dense part of the bones is the outer layer. It contains lots of calcium, a chemical we get from food. Teeth contain lots of calcium, too.

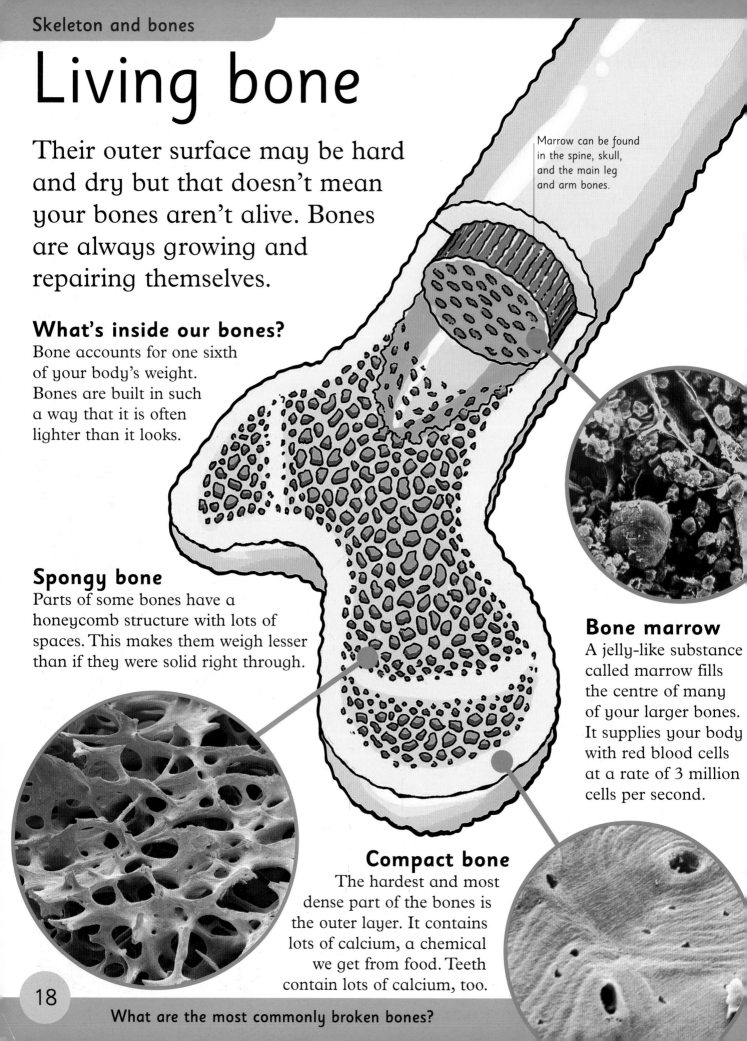

18

Broken bone

Bones are strong and flexible enough to cope with a lot of pressure, but, as this X-ray shows, they sometimes break. Luckily, they can heal themselves.

If the ends of the broken bones slip apart, they must be repositioned by a doctor so that they can heal properly.

On the mend

New cells form at each end of the broken bone, closing the gap between them. It takes about six weeks for this to happen.

Your bones continue to grow until your late teens.

Padded clothes help protect bones from sudden impact.

Looking after your bones

Calcium from milk and cheese is needed to build strong bones. Weight-bearing exercise, such as walking, climbing, or skating helps to strengthen bones.

Picture detective

Take a look through the Skeleton and Bones pages and see if you can identify where these bony bits come from.

Turn and learn

Skeleton:
pp. 12-13
Skin and nails:
pp. 70-71

Fingers, wrists, arms, and collarbones.

Bone and cartilage

When you were a baby, you were tiny. Slowly, as you get older and bigger, your bones do a clever trick. Not only do they grow, but they also change.

Making bones

Babies' bones are made out of a soft and bendy material called cartilage. Slowly, this hardens and turns into bone.

 Baby bones are entirely made of soft, growing cartilage.

 Adolescent bones are mostly bone, with a small amount of cartilage.

 Adult bones stop growing. Most no longer contain cartilage.

Stick out your ears!

Your ears are made of cartilage, not bone. They are strong, but much more bendy than your bony bits.

More, less

You've got more bones than your mum or dad! You were born with over 300 "soft" bones, but as you get older, many fuse together. By the time you're 25, you'll have 206 fully formed bones.

Baby's hand

This cross-section of an ear shows that the cartilage sits between two layers of skin.

Which foods are rich in calcium, the mineral you need to grow healthy bones?

Child's
hand

Adult's
hand

Bone shows up as
purple in these X-rays.

Taller, shorter

Between each bone in
your spine are small discs of
cartilage. During the day, these
get squashed, and when you rest at
night they spread out again. This
means you're a little bit taller in
the morning than in the evening.

Cartilage
coats the ends
of these bones.

The pads of
cartilage get
squashed from
standing up
and stretch back
out while you're
lying down.

Smooth joints

The ends of neighbouring
bones are covered in smooth
cartilage. That way, they
can glide against each other
when you move.

21

Moving joints

Joints are the places where bones meet. Different kinds of joints allow you to move in different ways.

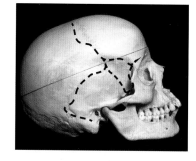

Hinge joint
Your knee can bend in the middle, but it can't swing from side to side. This joint has a hinge like the one that allows you to open and close a door.

Fixed joints
The bones that make up your skull start to join up soon after you are born. Once they have fused, none of them allow movement except the hinged jaw joint.

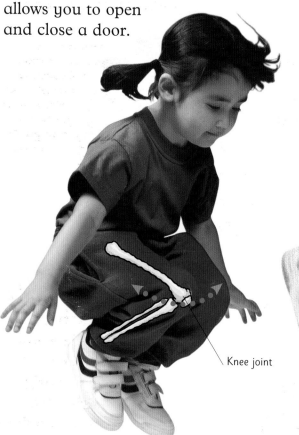

Knee joint

Ball and socket
Your hips are ball and socket joints. They allow you to move your legs in all directions and even to turn them. You also have a ball and socket joint in each shoulder.

There are 19 moveable joints in your hand, not counting the ones in your wrist!

What is tennis elbow?

Bendy bits

Different sorts of joints all over your body keep you moving.

Neck bones feature a pivot joint that allows your head to turn.

Wrists have a joint that allows them to turn but not to go right around.

Ankles contain different joints for up and down and side to side movement.

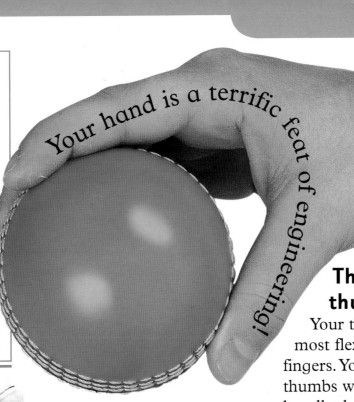

Your hand is a terrific feat of engineering!

Thank your thumbs

Your thumb is the most flexible of your fingers. You rely on your thumbs whenever you handle delicate objects.

This woman has stretchy muscles and ligaments that allow her spine to bend further than most people can manage.

Hip hooray

Joints, particularly knee and hip joints, sometimes wear out in old age. When this happens, doctors can remove the worn-out joint and replace it with an artificial one.

Ligaments

Bands of tissue called ligaments act like elastic. They hold your bones together, yet allow you to move.

Ligament

Bone

Your elbows have a hinge joint for bending, and a pivot joint so they can turn.

Fabulously flexible

People whose joints are particularly flexible are called "double-jointed". The condition can run in families, but people who are double-jointed must practise if they want to keep their ligaments stretchy.

23

The body's muscles

Every time you move, you use muscles. Muscles make you walk, blink, and smile. Some muscles work without you thinking about them, but others need to be told to move. They all work by shrinking, which makes them pull or squeeze.

Pulling strings

About 650 of your muscles are wrapped around the bones of your skeleton. They move your body by pulling on the bones. Together they form the muscle system.

Smooth muscle cells are short with pointed ends.

Smooth muscle

This type of muscle makes things move inside your body. It mixes food in your stomach and pushes food through your intestines.

Heart muscle

When you put your hand on your chest, you can feel your heart beating. Your heart is a strong muscle that squeezes blood around your body.

Heart muscle cells are stripy with oval blobs.

Skeletal muscle

Skeletal muscles pull on bones to change the shape of your skeleton and move your body. These muscles are voluntary, which means you can use thought to control them.

Skeletal muscle cells are long and threadlike.

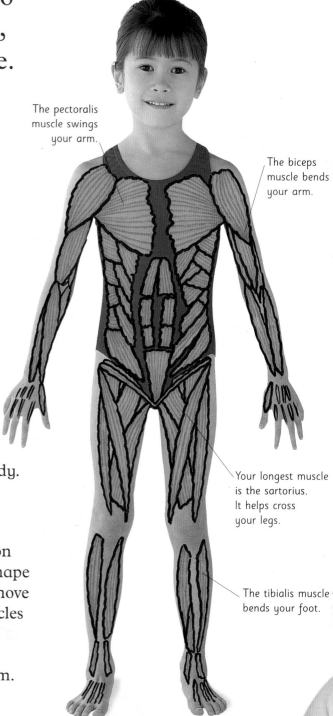

The pectoralis muscle swings your arm.

The biceps muscle bends your arm.

Your longest muscle is the sartorius. It helps cross your legs.

The tibialis muscle bends your foot.

What weighs more: all your bones or all your muscles?

Muscle magic

Muscles have hundreds of uses. They make up about a third of your body weight.

Your **largest muscle** is the muscle in your buttock which is used for sitting and walking.

Your **fastest muscle** is the one which makes you blink. It works up to five times a second.

Ear muscles can be controlled by a few people to wiggle their ears.

A fake **smile** uses different muscles from a real, involuntary smile.

Who's in charge?

You use hundreds of muscles when you run and jump. Your brain controls them all, a bit like a conductor controlling an orchestra. It sends signals along nerves to every muscle, saying exactly when to work and when to rest.

Turn and learn

Making sounds:
pp. 64-65
How intestines push food:
pp. 88-89

Hundreds of muscles work in a carefully controlled sequence when you jump in the air.

Tongue twister

Your tongue contains at least 14 different muscles that make it super flexible. It can reach anywhere in your mouth to pull and push bits of food. Its acrobatic movements are also vital to speech.

How muscles work

Muscles work by contracting, which means they shorten. As a muscle contracts, it pulls. The larger the muscle, the more powerfully it pulls.

When the biceps muscle contracts, it pulls your forearm and bends your arm.

When the triceps muscle contracts, it straightens your arm.

Working in pairs

Muscles can pull but not push. They work in pairs that pull in opposite directions. When one muscle pulls, its partner relaxes.

Your forearm contains pairs of muscles that move your hand and fingers back and forth.

Fibres in fibres

Skeletal muscles are made of cells called muscle fibres. Inside these are even finer fibres called myofibrils, which contract to make a muscle shorten.

A typical muscle

Bundle of muscle cells

One muscle cell

Myofibrils inside a muscle cell

Where is the body's smallest muscle?

Try raising your ring finger with your hand in this position. It's stuck because it's joined to the same tendon as the middle finger.

Middle finger
Ring finger

Tendons

Muscles are fastened to bones by tough bands called tendons. When you wiggle your fingers, you can see the tendons move on the back of your hand.

Making faces

Muscles in your face are attached to skin as well as bone. They pull the skin when you change your expression. You use about 17 muscles when you smile.

A floppy start

A newborn baby has little control over his head or neck muscles. It takes about a month before it can hold up its head, and six months for strong, steady head control.

Getting a stitch

If you run a lot, you may get a pain in your side. This is a stitch. Scientists aren't sure exactly why it happens but it might be because the muscles and ligaments in your abdomen are working too hard.

No rest

Muscles work all the time. They hold you upright – without them you would flop on the floor. Muscles also work when you are asleep, keeping your body firm and toned.

Muscle power

The more you use your muscles, the better they get. Active games and exercise make your muscles larger, stronger, and more flexible. They also help you keep going without tiring.

Stamina

If you have stamina, you can keep going for a long time without getting tired. Exercise that makes you feel out of breath, like running, improves your stamina.

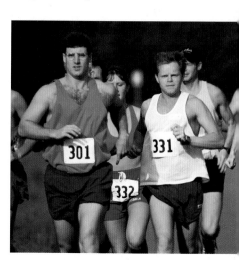

Flexibility

When you're flexible, your joints and muscles can move freely and your body can bend and straighten easily. Exercise that stretches your body, such as gymnastics or dancing, improves your flexibility.

This contortionist has made her body more flexible by doing exercises that stretch her back.

Strength

Pushing, pulling, and lifting make your muscles bigger and stronger. Bodybuilders lift heavy weights over and over again until their muscles are enormous.

You need strong muscles to win a tug-of-war.

Turn and learn

How your heart works: **pp. 50-51** Healthy food: **pp. 106-107**

What happens to muscles if you don't exercise?

Muscle food

To build strong muscles, you need a type of food called protein. Meat, fish, beans, milk, and eggs are rich in protein.

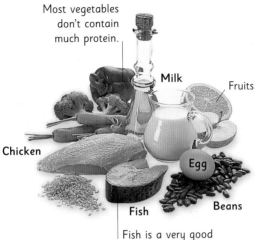

Most vegetables don't contain much protein.

Milk

Fruits

Chicken

Egg

Fish

Beans

Fish is a very good source of protein.

Ways to keep fit

Exercise is very good for your health. As well as making your muscles bigger, it strengthens your heart and lungs.

Walking to school, or going out for walks, builds strength and stamina.

Football is great for improving your flexibility and strength.

Swimming strengthens your heart muscle and builds stamina.

Cycling strengthens your leg muscles and builds up stamina.

Dancing keeps your body supple and helps build strength.

Body heat

This picture shows the heat of a man's body. Muscles make heat when they work hard, which is why exercise makes you hot. On cold days, your muscles try to warm you up by shivering.

They get small and weak.

Headquarters

The brain is the body's control centre. It is a complicated organ that works very quickly, a bit like a brilliant, living computer.

Sense signals
The cerebrum is the main part of your brain. It gets and stores sense information and also controls your movements.

Cerebrum

Cerebellum

Brain stem

Clever calculator
The cerebrum is also responsible for thinking, speaking, and complicated tasks such as sums.

Whatever else you do, the brain stem makes sure your heart and breathing never stop.

Muscle control
Your cerebellum helps you to balance and move your muscles. You use this bit of your brain when you dance.

24 hours a day
Your brain stem works at the same rate whether you're awake or asleep.

Does your brain hurt when you have a headache?

Skull

Brain

In relation to the size of our bodies, humans have the biggest brains of any animal.

Brain box

Your skull is a bony shell that fits together like a jigsaw around your brain. Shock-absorbing liquid fills the space between the brain and skull.

Learning

When you learn to do something you create connections between cells in your brain. Next time you do it the connections are already there so it is easier.

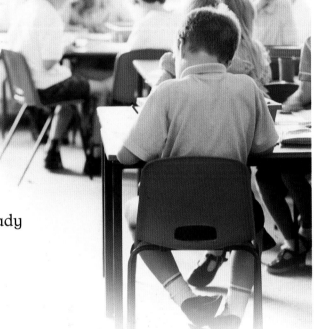

Short-term memory

Your short-term memory only holds information for about a minute. You use it to compare prices when you go shopping, or to remember a name when you meet someone new.

Long-term memory

Your name, phone numbers you know by heart, and skills such as riding a bike can be kept for many years in your long-term memory.

Picture detective

Take a look through the Brain and Senses pages and see if you can spot where these come from.

No, your brain can't feel pain but the muscles around your head can.

Network of nerves

All of the body contains nerve cells. These link up to form the network of nerves we call the nervous system. It transports messages between the body and the brain.

Quick as a flash

Nerve cells lie next to one another forming long chains. They pass messages to their neighbours – rather like a speedy relay race – to and from the brain.

A good night's sleep

Your body and brain slow down when you sleep, but they don't stop working. Your brain needs sleep to sort out the events of the previous day.

If you cross your legs and tap just below the knee, your knee jumps forwards even though your brain hasn't told it to move.

No need to think

You do some things without needing to think about them. These are called reflex actions and include blinking, coughing, and the

Brain

Spinal cord – the centre of the network

Brain cells viewed through a microscope.

Which is the longest nerve in your body?

Pain-killers

When you get a filling, the dentist gives you an anaesthetic. This drug stops nerves passing on pain messages for a short time.

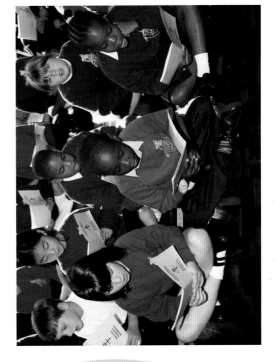

You've got 150,000 km (93,200 miles) of nerves in your body.

Pins and needles

Sitting cross-legged for a long time squashes the nerves in your legs. When you stand up, the nerves start to work again, producing a tingling feeling.

Messages travel faster than a high-speed train.

Messages

Your brain controls your body. It receives messages from all parts of your body and decides what to do.

Walking is the result of your brain telling your leg muscles to move.

Hunger is your stomach telling your brain that it's empty and you must eat.

Needing to urinate is a response to the message that your bladder is full.

Itching is an irritating feeling. Your body reacts by making you scratch.

Pain gets a very quick response. You move away from what's hurting you.

Blinking happens without you needing to think about it.

Breathing is automatic, too. It carries on even when you are asleep.

The one running from your big toe to the base of your spine.

Touchy feely

Your skin is in immediate contact with the world. Using your sense of touch allows you to tell if something is hot or cold, dull or sharp, rough or smooth, and wet or dry.

Merkel's disk responds to light touch and is sensitive to the texture of things.

Meissner's corpuscle senses light touch.

Things we can feel

Skin is packed with many sense receptors. Each sort responds to different sensations.

Warmth is detected by nerve endings quite close to the surface of the skin.

Cold sensors identify temperature. Extreme cold registers as pain.

Deep touch sensors enable you to grip things tightly.

Light touch sensors lie at the root of hairs on your arms and legs.

Vibrations from an electric drill trigger vibration sensors.

Tickly feelings result from a light and unexpected touch.

Sensitive fingertips are full of receptors and are able to tell coins apart.

Not worth noticing

Although your brain receives messages all the time, it filters out the less important ones. That's why you're not constantly aware of the clothes against your skin.

It feels slimy...

Ouch!

The body has its own system of alarm bells. Pain receptors warn us when a part of the body has been hurt or is about to be harmed.

This girl quickly moves her finger away from the thorn to stop the pain.

34

Free nerve endings respond to heat, cold, and pain.

Surface of skin

The Ruffini ending responds to firm or continuous touch.

Dermis

Under the skin
Dead cells form the surface of your skin. Sweat glands, hair follicles, and different types of sensory receptors lie below the surface.

The Pacinian corpuscle responds to firm pressure and vibration.

Fat

... and this message shoots off to the brain!

Braille was invented more than 150 years ago.

B I R D

Sensitive bits
Your skin contains more touch receptors than any other part of your body. But some areas are more sensitive than others.

Fingertips are packed with sensors, especially light pressure receptors.

Lips have very thin skin, which is good for detecting heat and cold.

Toes are very sensitive, but thick skin makes the heel less sensitive.

Reading by touch
Braille is a system that uses raised dots to represent letters and numbers. It was invented so that people with no eyesight would be able to read by feeling the page with their fingertips instead of looking at words.

hands on
Put one finger in cold water, one in hot, then put both in warm water. The water feels cold to the hot-water finger and hot to the cold-water finger.

About 3,000. That's roughly the same as on the whole of the trunk of your body.

Taste and smell

We need to eat and drink to survive, but taste and smell are what make these everyday activities so enjoyable.

Taste detector

Your tongue is a big muscle covered in lots of taste buds. These taste buds recognize different kinds of flavours, such as sweet and sour.

Different tastes

There are five types of taste – bitter, sour, salty, sweet, and umami.

 Some **bitter** foods, such as coffee, can be bad for you. Most poisons are bitter.

 Sour foods include lemon and vinegar. Food that has "gone off" tastes sour.

 Salt-detecting taste buds can be found on the lips as well as on the tongue.

 Sweet foods naturally attract us. Our first food – milk – is sweet.

 Umami is the savoury taste of foods like soy sauce and mushrooms.

10,000 taste buds are crammed in your tongue.

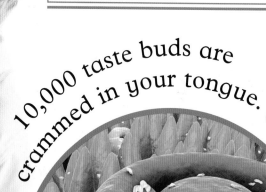

Taste buds in a papilla

hands on

Try putting sugar on different places on your tongue. It tastes sweeter in some places than others. Now try salt, lemon juice, and coffee.

Taste buds

Saliva in your mouth dissolves your food. The food washes over tiny bumps (called papillae) on your tongue. The taste buds lie inside some of these bumps.

How much saliva does an average person produce in a day?

Runny nose

When you have a cold, tiny hairs in your nose get clogged with mucus. This stops them from wafting smell particles deep into your nose, making it difficult to smell – and taste – things.

Your nose and mouth are linked at the throat.

Sensitive nose

Much of what we think of as taste is actually smell. The back of your nose is linked to your mouth so you can smell your food as you chew it.

Some people can recognize up to 10,000 different smells.

Smell receptors

Special cells deep inside your nose recognize scent particles floating in the air. These cells link directly to your brain.

37

Look out!

Sight is the body's main sense and the main way we learn about our surroundings. The eyes are delicate, but complex organs that enable us to see.

Wandering eyes

Six muscles control each eye. You use both eyes when you look at something, so your eyes move together.

Sclera (or white of the eye)

Iris

Pup

The middle of the eyeball is filled with fluid

The muscles surrounding your eyeball make precise movements so you can smoothly track moving objects.

An iris is as unique as a fingerprint

At night, our eyes could detect a lighted candle 1.6 km (1 mile) away.

Pupil

Eyelid

Iris

Sclera

Hidden away

Most of your eye nestles safely in its socket and is protected by pads of fat. On the outside, you can see the iris, pupil, and some of the sclera.

38

What is the sleep that collects in our eyes?

Tears are made behind each eyelid.

Tears drain into tear ducts. These link to your nose, which is why your nose runs when you cry.

Crying

Tear glands behind your eyes produce drops of salty fluid. When you blink, your eyelids sweep this fluid over your eyes to keep them clean. If something gets into your eye, or you feel strong emotions, the drops turn into floods of tears.

Safekeeping

Your eyes are fragile balls made of something like a watery jelly, so they need to be well protected.

Bone in your skull surrounds your brain and the backs of the eyes.

Eyebrows sit above your eyes and prevent sweat dripping into them.

Eyelids and **lashes** stop dust entering the eyes and then sweep it well away.

Your pupils change size on their own.

Enlarged pupils mean it's either dark or this person has seen something they like.

Pupil size

The pupil is the opening that controls how much light enters your eye. It's smaller in bright light to protect the nerve cells in your eye, and bigger in dim light to let more light in. It also gets bigger when you see something or someone you like.

Eye colour

The iris is the coloured part of the eye. All eye colours are produced by one substance, melanin. Lots of melanin results in brown eyes, less means a lighter shade.

Dust and mucus washed from our eyes as we sleep.

How we see

Inside your eye is a lens like the lens of a camera. Its job is to focus light on the back of your eye so you can see things clearly.

Light reflects off an object and enters your eye.

Optic nerve

The eye is filled with a semi-solid gel.

The retina contains cells that sense light.

The lens is clear and flexible. It focuses on things by changing shape.

The pupil is a hole that lets light into the eye.

An object

How your eye works

Light from an object enters your eye through the pupil. It passes through the lens, and makes an upside-down image on the retina at the back of your eye. Cells in your eye send messages down the optic nerve to your brain. Your brain flips the image back the right way round.

Seeing in colour

Your eyes contain millions of cells. Cone cells give you colour vision but don't work well in dim light. Rod cells work well in dim light but see everything in shades of grey.

What is an eye specialist who tests eyesight called?

Blurry vision

Sometimes an eyeball is the wrong shape. The lens cannot focus light on the retina and everything is blurry. Glasses make the light focus in the right place to make things clear.

Short eyeball

If you have a short eyeball, you will have difficulty seeing things close up. This is called long sightedness.

Long eyeball

It is difficult to see objects that are far away when your eyeball is too long. This is known as short sightedness.

Can you see a number? If not, you may be colour blind.

Colour blindness

Some people cannot tell certain colours apart, especially red and green. This is called colour blindness. It is more common in men than women.

Glasses bend the light entering your eye so it focuses on the retina.

hands on

👏 Close one eye and hold a finger in front of your nose. Open that eye and close the other one. The finger appears to move! Each eye sees things differently.

Contact lenses

These work like mini glasses and sit directly in front of the eye. They're a bit fiddly, but once they're in, you can't feel them at all.

Contact lenses are made of very thin plastic.

Eye to brain

Your brain works out what you're seeing by comparing the images it gets from your eyes to things you have seen in the past. Sometimes it can be fooled!

Your brain combines images from both eyes.

What can you see?
The dark blue in these pictures shows how much animals can see clearly. Light blue shows what they can see less well.

Humans have to move their heads to see clearly to the sides or look back.

Tigers see well to the front to help them find and catch their prey.

Zebras keep a look out for movements to the sides so they can avoid attack.

Ducks can see all the way behind them, even while facing forwards.

Chameleons see small areas clearly. They swivel their eyes to see all around.

The yellow areas are the parts of your brain that deal with information from your eyes.

Optic nerve

To the brain
Our eyes swivel around constantly, taking in sights and adjusting to focus on different things. The information they collect travels to the brain through the optic nerve at the back of the eyes.

Eyeball

Your blind spot is the part of the eye that can't see anything. It is where the optic nerve leaves the back of your eye.

What is it called when you look at something and think it's something else?

Tallest tower

Does the green tower look taller than the others? That's because it's farther along the track and we expect objects farther away from us to look smaller. The colours of the towers also affect the size they seem to be. In fact, all the towers are exactly the same size.

Finding your blind spot

Close your right eye and look directly at the star. Slowly bring the book to your left eye. You reach your blind spot when the circle disappears.

Recognizing objects

Your brain is very clever – it can recognize this car from different points of view. A computer would have to be taught that both these pictures are of the same object.

Certain patterns trick your eyes into seeing movement where there is none.

Do you believe your eyes?

Your brain helps your eyes to understand what they see. Sometimes you see things that aren't actually there.

You see a heart even though the edge of the shape isn't there because your brain uses the information it has to fill in the gaps.

Listen here

When you shout, you send out invisible sound waves through the air. Your ears pick up the waves and transmit the sound to your brain.

The speed of sound
We don't notice the slight delay between someone's lips moving and the sound actually reaching our ears. It's too fast!

How well can you hear?
Your hearing range is from the highest to the lowest notes that you can hear.

Adults have quite a small range compared to other animals.

Children hear higher notes than adults. Your range shrinks with age.

Cats, **dogs**, and **rabbits** can hear much higher notes than people.

Bats have excellent hearing. Their range is five times as large as ours.

Sound travels through the...

Headphones feed different sounds into each ear so you feel as if you're surrounded by instruments.

Why two ears?
Sounds normally reach one ear first and then the other. This helps our brains work out where sounds are coming from and how far away they are.

Why do we have ear wax?

Outer ear

What we call the ear is really just the part that we can see. Sounds are collected here, and funnelled inwards.

A little help

Partially deaf people may use hearing aids. These make the sounds entering the ear louder and easier to hear.

Middle ear

Sounds arriving here from the outer ear cause the eardrum to vibrate and set off movements in three tiny little bones.

.. air to your ear.

Outer ear

Ear canal

Bones

Cochlea

Middle ear

Inner ear

Ear drum

Tiny hairs are moved by sounds.

Signals travel along these nerves to the brain.

Inner ear

The bones moving cause vibrations in the liquid deep inside the ear. Tiny hairs in your inner ear pick up these vibrations in the liquid around them. The hairs are attached to nerves, which connect to your brain.

To protect the skin lining the ear canal, trap dust, and repel insects.

Balancing act

As well as hearing, ears help you balance. Sensors in your ears work with those in your eyes, muscles, joints, and feet to let your brain know your body's position.

The three semi-circular canals deal with balance.

Ear hole

Keeping track

Deep inside your ear are three tiny tubes filled with fluid. They detect the movements your body is making and let your brain know about them.

One tube is for forwards and backwards movements, another for up and down, and the third for side-to-side movements.

Watch your step!

Keeping your balance while walking along a narrow wall takes a lot of concentration. You are responding to information coming from your eyes, muscles, and ears at the same time.

A jelly-like knob floats in each tube. Inside it are sensitive hairs that detect movement.

The movements travel along the hairs, through a nerve, to the brain.

46

Motion sickness

Travelling in a car, boat, or plane can make you feel ill. Your eyes tell your brain that you're staying still in the vehicle, but your body says it can feel movement. This confusion is what causes motion sickness.

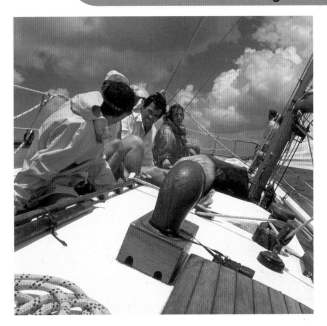

Your brain is the boss!

Muscle messages

When you move, sensors in your muscles send messages to your brain. If a movement isn't going right, your brain will make you do things differently.

The brain

hands on

First make sure there is nothing unsafe nearby for you to crash into. Then spin round and round and make yourself feel dizzy.

Why do you feel dizzy?

The liquid in the tubes of your ear is like water in a cup. When you spin, it continues to slosh around for a while even after you've stopped. Your brain gets confused about which way round you are, and you feel dizzy as a result.

The more you practise, the better you will be at balancing.

Yes, but it can take a couple of days to learn how.

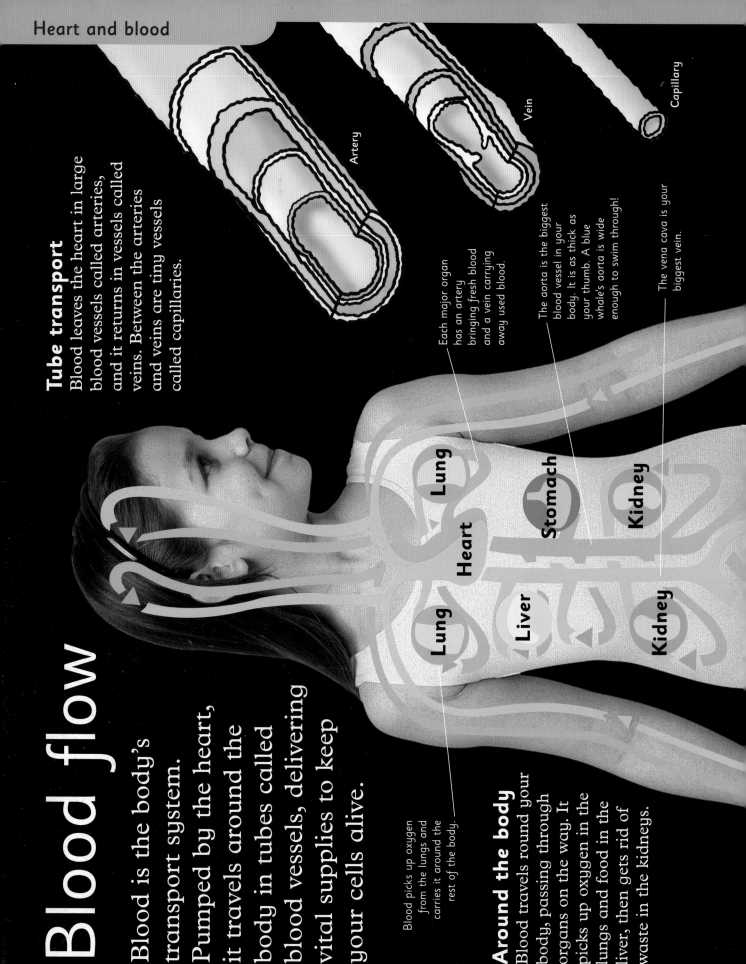

Tube transport

Blood leaves the heart in large blood vessels called arteries, and it returns in vessels called veins. Between the arteries and veins are tiny vessels called capillaries.

Artery

Vein

Capillary

Blood flow

Blood is the body's transport system. Pumped by the heart, it travels around the body in tubes called blood vessels, delivering vital supplies to keep your cells alive.

Each major organ has an artery bringing fresh blood and a vein carrying away used blood.

The aorta is the biggest blood vessel in your body. It is as thick as your thumb. A blue whale's aorta is wide enough to swim through!

The vena cava is your biggest vein.

Blood picks up oxygen from the lungs and carries it around the rest of the body.

Around the body

Blood travels round your body, passing through organs on the way. It picks up oxygen in the lungs and food in the liver, then gets rid of waste in the kidneys.

Lung

Lung

Heart

Liver

Stomach

Kidney

Kidney

When you cut yourself, what kind of blood vessel does the blood usually come from?

Capillaries

Arteries split into smaller and smaller branches. Eventually they turn into capillaries, which are finer than hairs. Capillaries lead into veins, which join together and get bigger on the way back to the heart.

Capillaries

Arteries

Veins

Artery

Vein

Your body has about 100,000 km (60,000 miles) of blood vessels

Turn and learn
Breathing in and out:
pp. 60-61
Air and oxygen:
pp. 62-63

From red to blue
The colour of blood depends on how much oxygen it contains.

Oxygen-rich blood in arteries is brilliant red.

Oxygen-poor blood in veins is dark, purplish red (shown blue on the diagram).

A capillary.

Boom boom

Your heart is a pump that pushes blood around your whole body. Each time your heart beats, it pumps out about a cupful of blood and refills for the next beat.

Where is it?

Your heart is in the middle of your chest, squeezed between the two lungs. You can feel it beating just left of the bone in the middle of your chest.

Double pump

Your heart is really two pumps in one. One half pumps blood through your lungs, and the other half pumps blood around the rest of your body.

Blood from most of the body coming through the vena cava

Blood going out to the body through the aorta

Blood going out to the lungs

Blood coming in from the lungs

One side pumps blood to the lungs...

Vena cava

Aorta

Blood coming from the body

Blood going out to the body

50

One-way system

To keep blood flowing one way only, your heart and most veins contain valves. Your heartbeat is the sound of valves shutting when your heart squeezes.

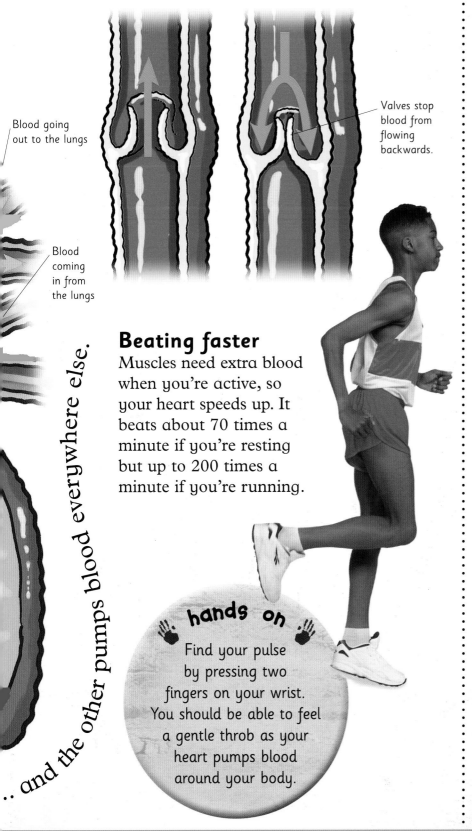

Blood going out to the lungs

Blood coming in from the lungs

Valves stop blood from flowing backwards.

... and the other pumps blood everywhere else.

Beating faster

Muscles need extra blood when you're active, so your heart speeds up. It beats about 70 times a minute if you're resting but up to 200 times a minute if you're running.

hands on

Find your pulse by pressing two fingers on your wrist. You should be able to feel a gentle throb as your heart pumps blood around your body.

Picture detective

Take a look through the Heart and Blood section and see if you can spot any of the cells and tissues below.

51

All about blood

Blood is a warm, soupy mixture of liquid and cells. The cells carry oxygen and fight germs, and the liquid carries nutrients to body cells and takes away waste.

Main ingredients

Blood contains three types of cells – red blood cells, white blood cells, and platelets. They float in a yellowish liquid called plasma.

A drop of blood

One drop of blood contains five million red blood cells, half a million platelet cells, 7,000 white blood cells, water, sugar, salt, hormones, vitamins, fat, and protein.

Yellow plasma makes up more than half of your blood.

White blood cells and platelets

White blood cells seek out and kill germs. They also eat up the dead cells that they meet.

Turn and learn

Fighting germs:
pp. 78-79
Air and oxygen:
pp. 62-63

Red blood cells make blood re

Red blood cells transport oxygen from your lungs to the rest of your body.

How long does a red blood cell live for?

Blood bank

One in ten people who go to hospital need extra blood, so hospitals keep a store of blood in a "blood bank". The blood is divided into separate supplies of cells and plasma.

Your blood type

There are four main types of blood, called blood groups. Your blood group affects who you can donate blood to.

People with blood **group A** can give blood only to people with A or AB.

People with blood **group O** can donate blood to almost anyone.

People with blood **group AB** can only give blood to others with AB blood.

People with blood **group B** can give blood only to people with B or AB.

White blood cells and platelets fight disease.

Platelets are cells that become sticky to make blood clot and form scabs.

How much blood?

The average adult has about 10 pints (5.7 litres) of blood, but a newborn baby has only a cupful.

The amount of blood in your body grows with you. By age 10 you have up to 4 pints (2 litres).

By a year old a baby has more than 1 pint (half a litre) of blood.

About four months.

53

Blood cells

Nearly half the cells in your body are blood cells. They wear out quickly, so you make three million new ones every second. Most are made in bone marrow, a jelly-like tissue in hollow bones.

Red blood cells

The most common cells in your body are red blood cells. They are circular with dimples in each side. Inside, they are packed with a red protein called haemoglobin, which carries oxygen.

White blood cell

Tiny tunnels

Red blood cells are soft and rubbery, so they can squeeze through tiny gaps. In the smallest blood vessels, they travel in single file. All the bumping and squeezing eventually wears them out.

Which cells in the human body contain the most iron?

Stick together

Platelets are tiny fragments of cells that help blood to clot. They cluster around breaks in blood vessels and grow spiky stalks that help them stick together.

Platelets stick together in a blood clot.

This white blood cell eats pus and germs.

This white blood cell crawls between other cells, looking for germs.

Soldier cells

There are lots of different white blood cells and they all help guard your body against invasion by germs. Some white blood cells creep along the walls of blood vessels and eat any germs they find. Others make chemicals that destroy germs.

Thicker blood

When people climb high mountains, their bodies make extra red blood cells to help them breathe in the thin mountain air. As a result, their blood gets thicker.

Pupils are normally black but they look red in photographs taken with a flash.

Seeing red

Have you ever seen pictures where a person's eyes seem red? If you take a picture with a flash, the light reflects off the red blood cells in the back of their eyes, making the pupils look red.

Red blood cells.

Bumps and cuts

Blood has the amazing ability to turn from liquid to solid in minutes and so help mend cuts in your skin.

Clotting

The moment you cut yourself, your blood starts turning solid, or clotting. The clot quickly plugs the broken blood vessels and stops them from leaking.

Caught in a net

The chemicals released by platelets cause tangled fibres to form in the liquid part of blood. The fibres trap blood cells, like fish in a net, forming a solid plug that gets bigger and bigger.

Tangled fibres trap blood cells.

Platelets in action

Platelets start the clotting process. They change shape to become stickier and cluster around the cut. At the same time, they release chemicals into the blood.

Platelets in the blood start to work as soon as you get a cut in your skin.

56

How long does a small cut take to stop bleeding?

Bloodsucker

A leech is a kind of worm that bites your skin and sucks out your blood. Leech saliva contains chemicals that stops blood from clotting. As a result, the cut keeps bleeding until the leech is full.

Leeches live in wet, swampy places. They often slip down people's shoes and bite their feet without being noticed.

Vampire bats and leeches can prevent blood from clotting.

First aid

A plaster can help a cut to heal by covering the skin and keeping out dirt. Plasters also stop you from scratching, which can make a cut worse.

Scabs

When a blood clot dries, it forms a scab. New skin slowly grows underneath the scab, repairing the wound. When the skin is ready, the scab becomes loose and drops off.

Scabs keep out germs while new skin grows.

Platelets stick to each other and to other blood cells, causing a clot to start forming.

After a few minutes, the clot is thick enough to stop blood escaping from the wound.

Bumps and cuts

Your body can naturally heal painful bumps and cuts of different kinds.

 A graze is a group of tiny cuts. It forms when something rough scrapes the skin quickly.

 Blisters are bubbles of liquid that form when skin is rubbed a lot. Don't pop them!

 Bruises are patches of blood under the skin. They change colour as they heal.

 Black eyes are bruises that form when blood pools under the skin around the eye.

Between three and eight minutes.

Hormones

A hormone is a chemical that changes the way part of your body works. Even tiny amounts of hormones are powerful. Some work slowly over years, but others have instant effects.

The pea-sized pituitary gland is just under your brain.

Growth hormone

Every day, your pituitary gland releases about eight microscopic doses of growth hormone, mostly when you're asleep. This hormone makes your bones and muscles grow.

The amount of growth hormone you make in one year is less than this tiny pinch of sugar.

Main gland

Hormones are made in parts of the body called glands. The most important is the pituitary gland in your brain. Its hormones control many of the other glands.

In their first year, children grow almost 30 cm (1 ft) taller.

Growing up

Toddlers and teenagers have very high levels of growth hormone, which is why they grow so quickly. Adults also make growth hormone, but the level falls with age.

What carries hormones around the body?

Control chemicals

Hormones are very important – they control many body processes.

 Oestrogen is the female sex hormone. It turns little girls into adult women.

 Testosterone is the male sex hormone. It turns little boys into adult men.

 Melatonin helps control the daily cycle of sleeping and waking.

 Glucagon raises the level of sugar in your blood, giving you energy.

 Parathyroid hormone tells your bones to release calcium into the blood.

The fright hormone

The hormone adrenaline makes you feel scared or excited. It works in an instant, preparing your whole body for sudden action in case you need to escape from danger.

Your brain becomes alert so you can think quickly.

Adrenaline makes your heart and lungs work harder. Your heart starts to pound and you gasp as your lungs take in extra air.

Lung

Heart

Glands above your kidneys release adrenaline.

Sugar control

The hormone insulin helps control the level of sugar in your blood. Some people don't make enough insulin and have to check their blood sugar level regularly. They have a disease called diabetes.

People with diabetes prick their skin to get a drop of blood, so that they can check how much sugar it contains.

Turn and learn

Growing up: **pp. 102-103** Sleep: **pp. 108-109**

Your hairs stand on end, making your skin tingle.

Adrenaline travels to your arms and legs and prepares the muscles for action.

The blood.

Air bags

We have to breathe all the time in order to supply our bodies with oxygen and to get rid of carbon dioxide. We use our lungs to do this.

Prepare the air

Before the air reaches your lungs, it travels through your mouth and nose and then goes down your windpipe. It gets warm and damp on its journey.

You breathe in through your nose or mouth.

This flap shut when you eat so that food can't go down your windpipe

The air travels down your windpipe.

Each lung is a spongy maze of tunnels.

When you breathe in, your lungs stretch out and take in lots of air.

When you breathe out, your lungs squash down, forcing all the air out.

The diaphragm is like a trampoline.

The muscle under your lungs is called the diaphragm. It moves up and down as you breathe.

In and out

Your ribs and diaphragm help you to breathe. Your lungs fill with air when you raise your ribcage, then empty out when you lower it. A muscle called the diaphragm helps you do this.

60

A helping hand

Some newborn babies have trouble breathing. They are put into an enclosed cradle called an incubator. Extra oxygen is pumped into the incubator for them.

Picture detective

Take a look through the Lungs and Breathing pages and see if you can identify where these images come from.

The view from the bottom of your windpipe.

Windpipe

Air from your mouth and nose enters your windpipe, which goes down your throat into your chest. Then it splits into two passages – one for each lung.

The alveoli are surrounded by tiny blood capillaries to take the oxygen round the body.

Air sacs

Your lungs are full of tunnels ending in tiny air sacs called alveoli. Here, oxygen from the air passes into your blood. Your blood carries oxygen around every part of your body.

About 23,000.

Air and oxygen

The air you breathe contains a life-giving gas called oxygen. Oxygen helps your cells get their energy from food. They would die within minutes if you stopped breathing

Oxygen

During the day, trees take in carbon dioxide from the air and give out oxygen.

Oxygen from trees
Trees help to clean the air by filtering out pollution. They also make oxygen, which they release through their leaves.

Carbon dioxide

You normally take about 20 breaths per minute – more if you're exercising.

It's better to breathe in and out through your nose than your mouth, specially while you're exercising.

What is in air?
Air is all around you, but you can't see, smell, or taste it. You can feel it when the wind blows.

Turn and learn
Cells – the body's building blocks:
pp. 8-9

Puffed out
Breathing heavily gives your body extra oxygen so it can work harder. You feel puffed out and pant when your lungs can't supply your body with oxygen quickly enough.

What is the kiss of life?

Airless places

Not every place has air to breathe, so sometimes people carry their own.

Fires burn up oxygen and produce thick, poisonous smoke.

Mountain tops have thin air with little oxygen.

Space and planets near Earth have no air to breathe.

Water contains oxygen, but humans cannot breathe it.

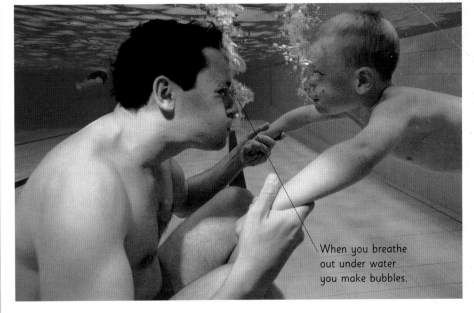

When you breathe out under water you make bubbles.

Hold that breath!

People can spend a few moments under water without breathing. Most people can manage about a minute, but the world record is around six minutes.

On a cold day you can see the water in your breath turn to steam as it meets the air.

You need to be able to control your breathing to blow up a balloon.

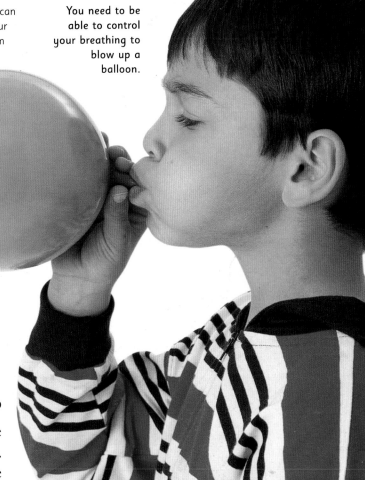

Wet air

Have you noticed that when you breathe onto a window or a mirror it becomes wet? That's because the air you breathe out is slightly damp.

How much air?

You take in about half a litre (0.8 pints) of air with each breath. If you breathe in deeply, you can take in about 3 litres (5 pints) in one gulp.

A way of helping someone who has stopped breathing by blowing into their mouth.

Making sounds

Humans can make many more sounds than other creatures. Because the shape of your face affects your voice, your voice is unique.

You can speak, whisper, hum, and shout!

Voice box
Your voice box has two jobs. You use it to make sounds, and to seal off your windpipe when you eat so you don't choke.

Open vocal cords

Closed vocal cords

Vocal cords
Inside your voice box are two flaps called vocal cords or folds. You make sounds by pushing air between them, causing them to vibrate. Fast vibrations produce high sounds, slower ones, low sounds.

Adam's apple
During puberty, a boy's voice box grows bigger, giving him a deeper voice. You can sometimes see it bulging at the front of the throat. It is known as the Adam's apple.

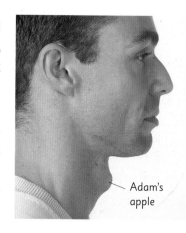

Adam's apple

Air supply
You use the air coming out of your lungs to produce sounds. So it's difficult to speak when you're breathless.

Why do babies and children have higher voices than adults?

Loud sounds

The harder air is forced out of the lungs, the louder the sound. So when a baby takes a big gulp of air, you can expect a really big cry!

Shaping words

The air coming from the lungs is shaped by the tongue, cheeks, and lips to form specific sounds.

 Oo is made by pursing your lips and pushing them out.

 Ah sounds are made with a low tongue and a wide open mouth.

 Ee is made by stretching your lips and keeping your tongue up high.

Snoring

Sometimes, when people sleep, the fleshy parts at the back of the nose and throat vibrate as they breathe. This rattling is called snoring. It can also happen when you have a cold.

A didgeridoo is a wind instrument.

Making music

You control your breath when you speak, but you need really excellent breath control to sing or play a wind instrument.

Turn and learn
Puberty:
pp. 102-103
Body language:
pp. 112-113

They have shorter vocal cords, which vibrate faster, producing higher sounds.

Ah-choo!

You need to keep your airways
clear to breathe at all times.
If something gets into your
airways, you have to get
it out pretty quickly!

A single sneeze can send 100,000 germs into the air!

Sneezing

Sneezes are a quick way to get rid
of unwanted particles that you have
accidentally breathed into your nose.

66

Gulp!

The sticky mucus (snot) in your nose and airways traps dust and dirt in the air that you breathe. Every day you swallow about a glass of the stuff.

Usually the flap is up, holding your windpipe open.

The flap closes when you swallow.

Safety catch

Unlike other animals, human beings use the throat both for eating and breathing. The epiglottis is a small flap of cartilage that shuts off your windpipe when you swallow so that food can't accidentally go down it and choke you.

Nose hairs

The tiny hairs in your nose work like brooms to sweep out any particles that you've breathed in. They get trapped in mucus and are swept along to be swallowed down your throat.

hands on

Yawning is catching! Is there anyone nearby? Give a yawn and see if you can start a yawning epidemic!

Coughing

Irritating particles that have entered your throat are thrown out when you cough. Coughing uses your vocal cords, which is why a noise comes out with the cough.

Hiccups

Sometimes your diaphragm suddenly tightens, causing air to rush into your lungs. This makes your vocal cords snap closed with a "hic". Hiccups seem to happen for no reason.

Yawning

Nobody knows why we yawn but we do know one effect of yawning: more oxygen in the lungs. It seems we yawn to perk ourselves up when we're feeling tired or bored.

No, because the nerves that control sneezing are relaxed at that time.

All wrapped up

Skin covers your whole body. It protects you from germs, water, and sunshine, and helps keep your body at the right temperature.

The skin on your eyelids is the thinnest on your body.

Two layers

Your skin has two main layers. The top one – the one you can see – is called the epidermis. Underneath is the dermis, where there are nerves and blood vessels.

There are flat cells on the surface of your skin. These are made from a tough material called keratin. When the cells die, they dry out and flake off.

Skin cells lower down replace the dead ones that flake off.

Skin is a sort of stretchy overcoat.

Waterproof seal

Skin stops water getting into your body when you have a shower or go for a swim. It also stops fluids escaping from inside you.

Magnified skin flakes

Heavy load

Skin is the heaviest single part of your body. It can weigh as much as a bag of shopping.

House dust

Dust is mostly made of dead skin. Dust mites feed on this skin. They live in beds, pillows, and carpets.

Dust mites aren't really this big! They're so small, you can't see them without a magnifying glass.

The thickest skin on...

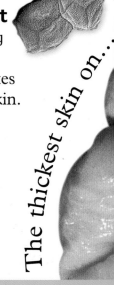

How many dead skin flakes fall off every day?

Sweat

Sweat pore

Sweat gland

If you uncurled
a sweat gland,
it could be over
1 m (3 ft) long.

Skin colour

The colour of your skin is affected by a
substance called melanin. The more melanin
you have, the darker you will be. When you are
outside in the sun, your body produces extra
melanin to protect your skin. This melanin
makes your skin darker and you get a suntan.

... your body is on the soles of your feet.

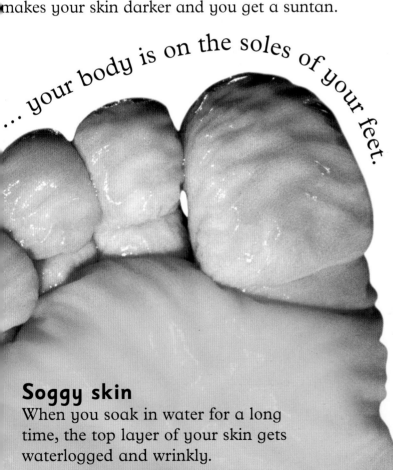

Cooling down

When sweat dries on your
skin, it helps to cool you
down. Sweat comes from
coiled tubes under the
surface. It gets out
through tiny holes
called pores.

Soggy skin

When you soak in water for a long
time, the top layer of your skin gets
waterlogged and wrinkly.

At your fingertips

Nails work with skin to protect your body. They stop you hurting the ends of your fingers and help you to pick things up.

Your fingertips have the most sensitive skin on your body.

Arch

Loop

Whorl

get mucky
Roll the soft part of your fingertip on an ink pad. Now roll your inky fingertip on a piece of paper. The mark you make is your very own fingerprint.

Fingertip patterns
Fingertips are covered with swirly ridges that help you grip things. These are called fingerprints. Everyone has different fingerprints with different patterns such as arches, loops, or whorls.

The skin around your joints is loose and saggy so you can bend them easily.

On the surface
To the naked eye, your hand looks smooth and solid. However, under a microscope, you can see the flaky, dead skin.

Sweat leaves almost invisible marks on all the surfaces you touch.

Police use fingerprints to help catch criminals.

Folds and flakes of dry, dead skin.

Why do you get white spots on your nails?

Nails grow from a root under your cuticle.

Cuticle

Fat

Bone

When you look at nail keratin close up, it has lots of flaky layers.

The inside story

Although nails are much harder than skin or hair, they're made from the same basic material. It is called keratin.

Our nails are like animals' claws.

Family connections

Like humans, birds and animals have body parts that are made of keratin.

Claws look like nails, but they are stronger and sharper.

Beaks are very hard so birds can tear food and crack seeds.

Holding on

It would be difficult to hold heavy things if you didn't have fingernails. They help to make your fingertips straight and strong. The other reason you have fingernails is so you can scratch when you're itchy!

Nail growth

Nails start to grow before you're born, and they carry on growing your whole life. They grow quicker on your hands than on your feet.

Horns contain different kinds of keratin. Rhino horns are made of hair keratin.

71

These spots mean the new nail has been banged or knocked.

Fairly hairy

Hair is mostly made of keratin, just like skin and nails. You have about 100,000 hairs on your head and millions more on your body.

Hair close-up

Each hair is covered with scales that overlap like roof tiles. This makes the hair strong and protects it. Hair is dead tissue, which is why it doesn't hurt to cut it.

Hair grows for up to seven years before it falls out.

What's your hair like?

Hair grows out of tiny pockets or follicles. The shape of these pockets controls whether hair is straight, wavy, or curly.

Like moulds, follicles shape each strand of hair. Straight hair grows out of straight follicles.

Slightly curvy follicles produce wavy strands of hair.

Head hair

Lots of body heat escapes from your head. The hair there, which is usually long and thick, keeps your head warm. Fine hairs cover every other part of you, except the palms of your hands, soles of your feet, and your lips.

How many hairs do you lose from your head every day?

Smooth surface

Some men lose their hair as they grow older. In fact, the hair still grows, but it is shorter and falls out more easily. A few people are born without any hair at all – not even eyelashes.

Colour chart

Hair, like skin, gets its colour from a chemical called melanin. If you have no melanin in your hair, it will be white – if you have lots, it will be jet black.

Brrrr...

When you're cold, tiny muscles pull your body hair upright. When the muscles pull, they make little ridges called goose pimples.

Goose pimple

Follicles that are very swirly in shape produce tightly curled hair.

Good food

If your head is itchy, you may have head lice. These creatures cling to your hair and suck blood from your scalp. When you play with friends, the lice crawl from one head to another. These fussy bugs like clean heads best.

73

Germs

Your body is a walking zoo. It's covered with bugs that feed and breed on you but are mostly too small to see. Many do no harm, but some, called germs, make you ill when they get inside you.

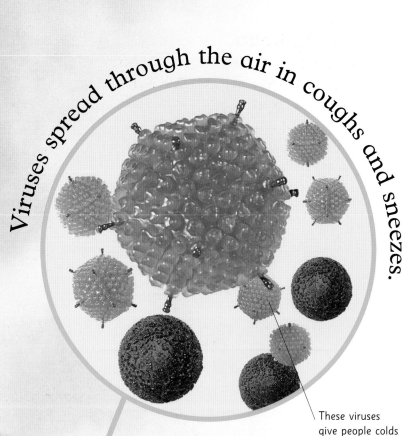

Viruses spread through the air in coughs and sneezes.

These viruses give people colds or the flu.

Vile viruses

Viruses are not actually alive. They get into cells and force the cells to make new copies of them. Viruses can cause colds, flu, measles, mumps, and warts.

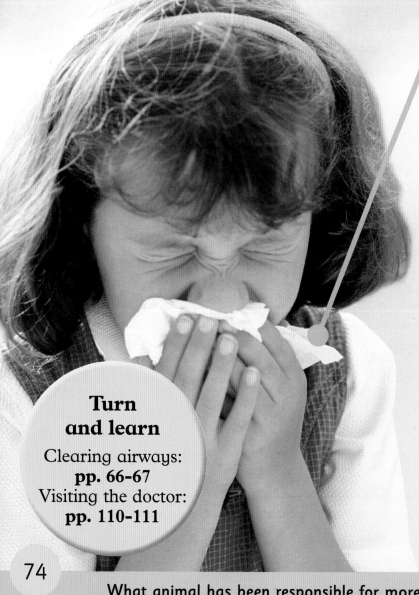

Turn and learn

Clearing airways:
pp. 66-67
Visiting the doctor:
pp. 110-111

Verucca

A verruca (wart) is a patch of thickened skin caused by a virus. The virus often spreads from person to person in places where people walk barefoot, such as swimming pools.

What animal has been responsible for more human deaths than any other?

Beastly bacteria

Most germs are bacteria (though not all bacteria are germs). When bacteria get into cuts, they cause swellings or sores. Certain types cause deadly diseases if they get into your lungs or stomach.

Your hand leaves bacteria on anything you touch.

Billions of bacteria

There are more bacteria on your skin than there are people in the world. Most do little harm, and some actually protect you from other germs. If you touch rotten food or faeces, your hands will pick up more dangerous bacteria.

Big bugs

Creatures much bigger than bacteria or viruses also feed on your body and can make you sick.

Giardia live in intestines and spread in dirty water. They cause diarrhoea.

Threadworms live in the large intestine and spread on dirty fingers.

Follicle mites live in the roots of most people's eyelashes and do little harm.

Mosquitos suck people's blood and spread germs that cause deadly diseases.

Fungi

Some germs are fungi (related to mushrooms). Tinea (ringworm) is a type of fungus that grows through skin like a plant, sending out long thin shoots.

The tinea fungus

The mosquito, because it injects germs into the body when it sucks blood.

Body defences

Although you can't see them, germs are always landing on your body and trying to get inside it. Your body has lots of clever ways of keeping them out.

Poison tears

Germs that land on your eyes are washed away by tears, which come from glands above your eyes. Tears contain the chemical lysozyme, which kills bacteria by making them burst open.

You make about 1 litre (2 pints) of saliva a day.

Saved by spit

The liquid in your mouth is called saliva. As well as helping you digest food, saliva protects your mouth, tongue, and teeth from attack by bacteria.

Earwax flows slowly out of your ears all the time, flushing out dirt and germs.

Sticky business

Germs get into your lungs when you breathe in. They get trapped in a sticky liquid called mucus, which lines your airways. Tiny beating hairs continually push the mucus up to your throat to be swallowed.

76

Which is your largest defensive organ?

Acid attack

Glands inside of your stomach make acid, which kills germs you've swallowed. Your digestive system then breaks down the germs along with your food.

Yuk!

The feeling of disgust protects you from germs. Anything that smells revolting or looks horrible is probably full of germs. Disgust stops you from touching it.

Turn and learn

Eyes:
pp. 38–39
Digesting food:
pp. 88–89

Slimy guts

The inside of your intestines are covered with slimy mucus, which stops germs from getting into your blood. Your large intestine also contains millions of "friendly" bacteria, which prevent other germs from growing.

Your skin.

Fighting germs

If germs break through your outer defences and invade your tissues, your body fights back. The cells of your immune system hunt and destroy germs. This system also remembers germs and protects you from them in the future.

Antibodies attacking germs.

Antibodies
Some white blood cells make chemicals called antibodies. These stick to the surface of germs, telling other body cells to attack.

Antibody

Killer cells
White blood cells called macrophages kill germs by swallowing them. When a macrophage finds a germ, it stretches out, wraps around the germ, and pulls it inside. Digestive juices then destroy it.

This germ is being swallowed.

This white blood cell is called a macrophage.

Heating up
Your body gets hotter when it fights germs, which gives you a high temperature.

How many tonsils do you have?

Lymph system

Fluid continually leaks out of your blood vessels and tissues. It returns to the blood through tubes called lymph vessels. Dotted along these are swellings called nodes, which filter out germs.

Extra protection

Doctors protect you from germs with vaccines. Vaccines contain weak or dead germs that your immune system learns to attack. If the real germ ever gets inside you, your immune system remembers it and attacks very quickly.

Super milk

Breast milk contains germ-killing antibodies that protect babies from disease. During the first few days of a baby's life, the mother makes a special milk called colostrum, which is packed with antibodies.

The swellings in lymph vessels are called lymph nodes.

Tonsil

Tonsils

At the back of your mouth are several patches of tissue called tonsils. They are full of white blood cells that fight germs in your throat. However, the tonsils sometimes fill with germs themselves and have to be removed.

Two main ones and four smaller ones.

Allergies

An allergy happens when your body mistakes a harmless substance for a germ and overreacts to it. Food, plants, dust, pets, and many other substances can cause allergies.

Allergens

A substance that triggers an allergy is called an allergen.

Wasp stings can kill people who are allergic to them.

Antibiotic medicines can give allergic people a rash on the skin.

Hair and **skin** from pets can cause an allergy very similar to hayfever.

Moulds grow in damp places. Their powdery spores can cause asthma.

Biological washing powder can cause a skin reaction.

Who gets allergies?

If you grow up in a large family or on a farm, your immune system will get lots of practice against germs. Some experts think this makes you less likely to get allergies.

Dust mites are related to spiders and have eight legs.

Mouth

Dust mites

Millions of these tiny beasts, which are smaller than full stops, live in your home. They feed on dead skin. Their microscopic faeces are a major cause of asthma.

What's the most common type of allergy?

Skin allergies

If you touch a thing you're allergic to, itchy red spots may appear on your skin. Poison ivy plants, make-up, jewellery, and clothes can cause skin allergies.

Poison ivy

Skin allergies cause itchy red spots that can look just like a nettle rash.

Pollen

A very common cause of allergy is a powdery dust called pollen, which is made by flowers. Pollen floats through the air and enters our bodies as we breathe.

Hayfever can make your eyes swollen, watery, and red.

Food allergies

Foods that cause allergies include strawberries, nuts, seafood, and eggs. These can give an allergic person a skin rash, a runny nose, a sore mouth, nausea, or diarrhoea.

Peanuts can be deadly to people with a nut allergy.

Hayfever

People who are allergic to pollen have hayfever. When they breathe in lots of pollen, their noses run and their eyes get sore. Hayfever is worst in spring and summer, when grass flowers release lots of pollen into the air.

Inhalers squirt out medicine in a spray, helping people with asthma to breathe.

Asthma

People with asthma can find it hard to breathe. Their chests feel tight and their breathing becomes wheezy. Asthma can be caused by an allergy to dust mites, cat hairs, or other substances in air.

81

Hayfever.

Digestive system

Food is made up of large, complicated chemicals that your body has to break into small chemicals that your blood can absorb. This process is called digestion.

Physical digestion

Some parts of your digestive system mash up food physically, just like a food processor does. Your mouth breaks food into chunks. Your stomach then churns these around until they form a slushy liquid.

When you swallow, food passes down a tube called the oesophagus.

Tube journey
Your digestive system is really just a long, tangled tube. Food travels about 9 m (30 ft) as it passes from start to finish.

Turn and learn
Taste and smell:
pp. 36-37
What's in food:
pp. 106-107

Liver

The Venus flytrap catches insects and digests them using enzymes.

Dragonfly

Large intestine

Venus flytrap

Chemical digestion
Many digestive organs make juices that break down the chemicals in food. The juices contain enzymes, which turn large food molecules into small molecules.

Small intestine

Rectum

82

Digesting a meal

A large meal takes a day or more to pass through your digestive system. Different digestive organs make enzymes that work on different parts of the meal.

Bread starts to break down in your mouth.

The fat in fries starts to break down in the small intestine.

The fibre in vegetables isn't digested.

Meat starts to break down in your stomach.

Stomach

6pm
Food gets swallowed 10 seconds after it enters your mouth.

10pm
A meal spends about 4 hours in the stomach, but very rich food can spend twice as long there.

3am
The meal is slowly squeezed through your small intestine, sometimes causing loud gurgling noises.

The next day
Undigested leftovers reach the end of their journey about a day after you swallowed the food.

Your small intestine.

Picture detective

Take a look through the Digestive System section and see if you can spot any of the cells and tissues below.

83

Chew it over

We use our teeth to bite off and chew our food. During the course of your life, you will have two separate sets of teeth.

First teeth
Your first teeth start to grow when you're about six months old. The front teeth usually appear first.

Adult teeth
When you are six, your first teeth start to fall out. Adult teeth with deeper roots grow to replace them.

Wisdom teeth
Your back teeth are called wisdom teeth. They appear when you are 17 or older, and sometimes not at all.

False teeth
If you don't take care of your teeth, they will decay and fall out. Then you will need false teeth.

Types of teeth
Your mouth contains a selection of different types of teeth. Each type is designed to do a different job.

A child has 20 teeth; an adult has 32.

Molars at the back of your mouth have a flat edge so you can mash your food thoroughly.

Premolars roughly crush and grind your food. They are smaller than molars.

Canines grip and tear food using a single rounded point.

Incisors at the front of your mouth slice up chunks of food.

Roots
The part of the tooth below the gum is its root. Without roots, your teeth might break or fly out of your mouth if you bite down hard. The root is held in place by tiny fibres that connect to the jaw bone.

Root of a tooth

What is another name for your first teeth?

Brush twice a day to keep decay away.

Brush your teeth!

A sticky mixture of food and bacteria builds up on the surface of your teeth if you don't clean them properly. It is called plaque.

Decay

Bacteria in plaque makes an acid that can eat through tooth enamel and attack the blood vessels and nerves deep inside the tooth. This is called decay. It hurts, and the dentist may need to give you a filling.

The sugar in sweets sticks to your teeth, forming plaque. Plaque contains bacteria that causes teeth to decay.

Inside a tooth

Deep inside your teeth are lots of blood vessels and nerves. The nerves mean you can feel heat, cold, and pain.

Enamel

The hardest and toughest substance in your body is tooth enamel. It contains no living cells, so it can't repair itself if it is damaged.

Enamel

Gum

Blood vessels and nerves

85

From mouth to stomach

You start digesting food the moment you bite into it. As your teeth tear the food apart, enzymes in your spit begin to attack it chemically. By the time it reaches your stomach, your meal is unrecognizable.

Seen close up, your tongue is covered by tiny bumps and stalks that make its surface rough, which improves its grip.

Get a grip

Your tongue is a super strong, flexible bundle of muscles that pushes food against your teeth as you chew. It has a rough surface for good grip.

Mouth watering

The slimy liquid in your mouth is saliva. It moistens food to make it easier to chew and swallow. Saliva also contains an enzyme that breaks down starch, one of the main ingredients in bread, rice, and pasta.

Tongue

Uvula, a fleshy tissue at the back of the throat

What is the scientific name for burping?

This flap shuts off your nose when you swallow.

This flap closes your windpipe as you swallow.

Tongue

Swallowing

Swallowing is a reflex action, which means it happens automatically without you having to think about it. When your tongue pushes food to the back of the mouth, the swallowing reflex begins.

When your stomach is empty, its stretchy wall is full of folds.

Stretchy stomach

Your stomach has a very stretchy wall so that it can expand to hold big meals. Glands in the wall make acid and enzymes that start digesting protein in meat.

Down the tube

Swallowed food gets pushed down a muscular tube called the oesophagus. The muscles work so well that you would still be able to swallow if you were standing on your head.

Food leaves your stomach through a small ring of muscle.

Stomach action

Your stomach's wall is made of muscles that squeeze in ripples to churn food about. When the food is ready to leave, the muscles squirt it out.

87

Eructation.

Inside the intestines

When food leaves your stomach, it enters a long, tangled tube. This has two parts. The first is your small intestine, which is long and narrow. The second is your large intestine, which is shorter but fatter.

Small intestine

The small intestine finishes off the job of digestion. Digested food soaks through its wall and enters the blood to be carried away.

Finger blobs

Tiny, finger-shaped blobs, known as villi, line the small intestine. They speed up the absorption of food.

Muscles push food through your intestines just like this hand pushes a ball along a stocking.

A squeezing action travels along the intestine in waves.

Pushed along

Your intestines use a special kind of muscle action called peristalsis to move food along. Rings of muscle in the intestines squeeze behind the food, pushing it forwards.

What is the total length of human instestines?

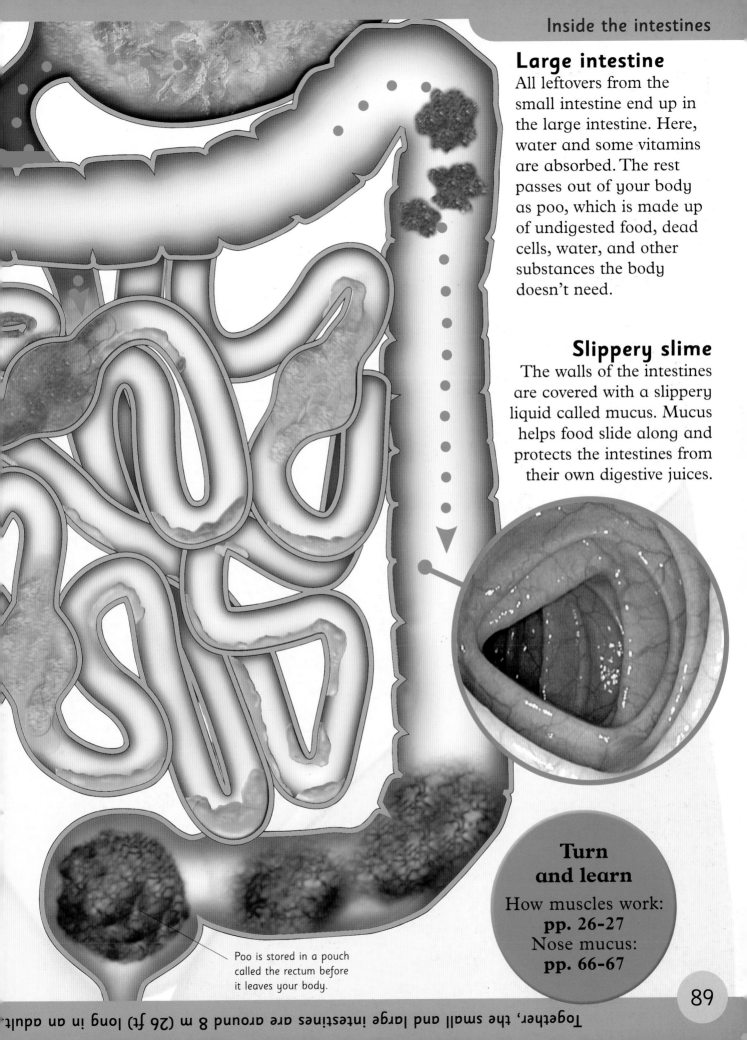

Large intestine

All leftovers from the small intestine end up in the large intestine. Here, water and some vitamins are absorbed. The rest passes out of your body as poo, which is made up of undigested food, dead cells, water, and other substances the body doesn't need.

Slippery slime

The walls of the intestines are covered with a slippery liquid called mucus. Mucus helps food slide along and protects the intestines from their own digestive juices.

Turn and learn

How muscles work: **pp. 26-27**
Nose mucus: **pp. 66-67**

Poo is stored in a pouch called the rectum before it leaves your body.

Together, the small and large intestines are around 8 m (26 ft) long in an adult.

Waterworks

Your body gets rid of waste chemicals and excess water by making urine. Urine comes from two organs called kidneys. They filter and clean blood as it flows through, removing chemicals that your body doesn't need.

Blood flows in and out of the kidneys through large blood vessels.

Urine dribbles away through a tube called the ureter.

The kidneys clean your blood.

The ureters carry away urine.

The bladder stores urine.

The urethra gets rid of urine.

Urinary system

Your kidneys, bladder, and the tubes connected to them make up your urinary system. The last part of the urinary system is the urethra. Urine comes out of this tube when you go to the toilet.

If you put your hands on your hips and your thumbs on your back, your kidneys are next to your thumb tips.

How long do your kidneys take to clean all the blood in your body?

Inside a kidney

The blood vessels entering your kidneys divide into smaller and smaller branches. These lead to a million tiny filtering units called nephrons.

Blood flows through a knot of tiny vessels.

Fluid passes out into a chamber.

The fluid leaves through this tube.

Inside a nephron

As blood flows through a nephron, fluids leave the blood vessel and pass into a long, looped tube. Useful chemicals are then reabsorbed into blood.

Balancing act

Kidneys keep the water level in your body perfectly balanced. If you drink too much, your kidneys make watery urine to get rid of any excess. When your body is short on water, your kidneys pass less of it into urine.

This part of the brain monitors the water level in blood.

When the water level is low, the pituitary gland in your brain releases ADH.

A low water level also triggers a feeling of thirst, making you drink.

ADH travels to your kidneys in your blood.

Your kidneys save water, making your urine stronger.

Water disposal

Here's how your body gets rid of water.

Urine makes up more than half of the water that leaves your body.

Breath contains over a quarter of the water your body gets rid of.

Sweat is only about one twelfth of the water leaving your body.

We also lose water through **poo** – it seems quite dry, but it is mostly water.

Water control

Your kidneys work together with your brain to control the water level in your body. When this level is low, your brain releases ADH – a hormone that makes your kidneys save water.

The stretchy bladder

All day long, a small stream of urine trickles out of each kidney. It collects in an organ called the bladder, which stores the urine until you go to the toilet.

Nappy rash

Babies sometimes get a rash under nappies. This happens because urine and poo collect in the nappy and make the skin sore.

Filling up

Your bladder stretches as it fills up. This sends a signal to your brain, making you want to go to the toilet.

Grapefruit

X-ray of a full bladder

X-ray of an empty bladder

Full stretch

An adult's bladder stretches from the size of a plum to the size of a grapefruit and can hold about 500 ml (1 pint) of urine. A child's bladder is about the size of an orange when it's full.

Orange

The muscles in the bladder's wall squeeze to push urine out.

Inside the bladder

The bladder has a waterproof lining to stop it leaking. Urine leaves through a tube called the urethra, which is normally kept shut by two muscles.

Plum

How much urine do you make each day?

What is urine?

Urine is made of water and waste chemicals. The main waste is urea, which your body makes when it breaks down protein. The colour of urine depends on how much you drink. If you drink lots of water, your urine will be pale.

The yellow colour comes from a chemical that forms when old blood cells are broken down.

Tubes called ureters bring urine from the kidneys.

This muscle opens automatically when the bladder is full.

Urethra

We have to learn to control this muscle.

Camel urine

Camels can last for months without water so they can survive in the driest deserts. They save water by making thick, syrupy urine that is twice as salty as seawater.

Camels store fat in their humps, which they use for energy.

Bladder control

In young children, the muscles that open the bladder work automatically. As children get older, they learn to control one of the muscles.

Potty training

Children gradually gain control of their bladder around the age of two, but they may still wet the bed while sleeping. By the age of four, most children can stay dry at night as well.

Toddlers have to learn bladder control.

93

Making a baby

You need a mother and a father to make a baby. The mother's body does most of the work, but the father also has an important job – his sperm joins with the mother's egg and a new life begins...

The first cells
After 36 hours, the cell has divided and made an exact copy of itself. These are the first two cells of a baby.

Eggs are the biggest cells in the human body. But they are still very small – 10 would fit across a pinhead.

Sperm look like tiny tadpoles. Under a microscope, you can see their tails wriggling as they swim.

By the time the baby is born, the fertilized cell will have become 100 trillion cells.

Sperm race
Millions of sperm swim towards the egg cell. Only one sperm can join with the egg to make a new cell.

What is another name for the uterus?

Divide again
You don't grow much in the first few days. The two cells divide to make four, then eight, and so on.

At three days
The cells have carried on dividing. There are now 16 cells and they are almost ready to plant themselves in the uterus.

The future you
Each cell is unique to you. Cells are full of instructions about what you will look like.

Where it all happens
The sperm fertilizes the egg in a tunnel, called a Fallopian tube. The fertilized egg moves down the tunnel towards the mother's uterus. The journey takes about five days.

The cells start dividing as they move down the Fallopian tube towards the uterus.

Millions of sperm from the father travel up here towards the egg.

This is the mother's ovary. It releases one egg every month.

This is the uterus. It is about the size of a pear and has muscular walls.

Arriving in the uterus
The ball of cells plants itself in the wall of the uterus. In this warm, dark place the baby will spend the next 40 weeks growing and developing.

Position of the uterus in the female body

95

Growing in the womb

By eight weeks old, the baby is no longer a bundle of cells. It looks like a tiny person and is called a "foetus". The foetus does not eat, drink, or breathe by itself. All its needs are taken care of by its mother.

Boy or girl?

Parents can find out about a baby's health and sex before it is born. A scanning machine shows the baby on a screen. This is many parents' first sight of their child.

Parents often choose not to find out their child's sex so they can have a surprise on its birthday.

Eight weeks old

Size of a strawberry

The foetus has eyes, a nose, lips, and a tongue. It lives in a protective bag of liquid and uses its tiny muscles to swim around gracefully.

Sixteen weeks old

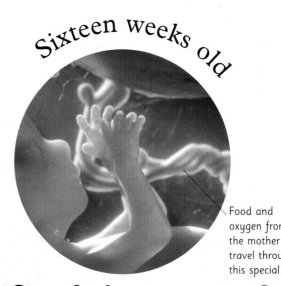

Food and oxygen from the mother travel through this special cord.

Size of a lemon

The foetus can make different faces, clench its fist, and suck its thumb. It can hear its first sounds but its eyes are not open yet.

Twenty weeks old

Size of a grapefruit

At 20 weeks, the foetus is getting more active. It is still quite small so there's plenty of room to kick around and turn somersaults.

When do we first start to dream?

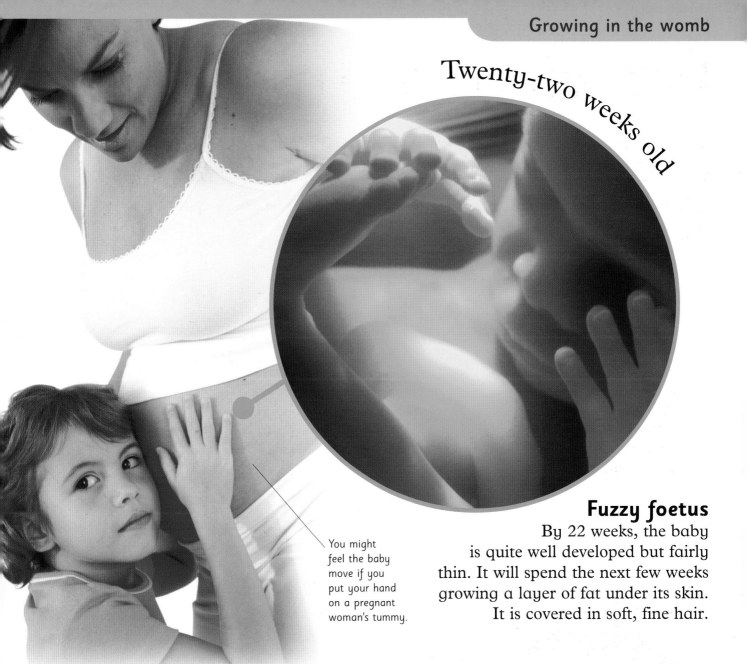

Twenty-two weeks old

You might feel the baby move if you put your hand on a pregnant woman's tummy.

Fuzzy foetus

By 22 weeks, the baby is quite well developed but fairly thin. It will spend the next few weeks growing a layer of fat under its skin. It is covered in soft, fine hair.

What's it like in there?

It is quite noisy in the womb with the sounds of the mother's heartbeat and stomach rumbles. The baby can also hear noises outside the womb and loud bangs may make it jump. It learns to recognize its mother's voice long before it is born.

Happy birthday!

At last, after around 40 weeks, the moment comes for the baby to be born. Newborn babies can breathe, suck, and swallow. They communicate by crying if they are hungry or feel uncomfortable.

Double trouble

There are two different types of twins – identical and non-identical. Identical twins mostly have the same genes. Non-identical twins are like any other brother or sister, so only half their genes are the same.

Types of twins

Twins are either identical or non-identical.

Identical twins are made when a fertilized egg splits into two separate cell clusters.

Fertilization occurs when a single sperm fuses with the egg.

The fertilized egg splits into two. We don't know what makes this happen.

Two cell clusters develop into two separate babies.

Non-identical twins are made when the mother releases two eggs instead of one.

Each egg is fertilized by a different sperm. Two babies then develop.

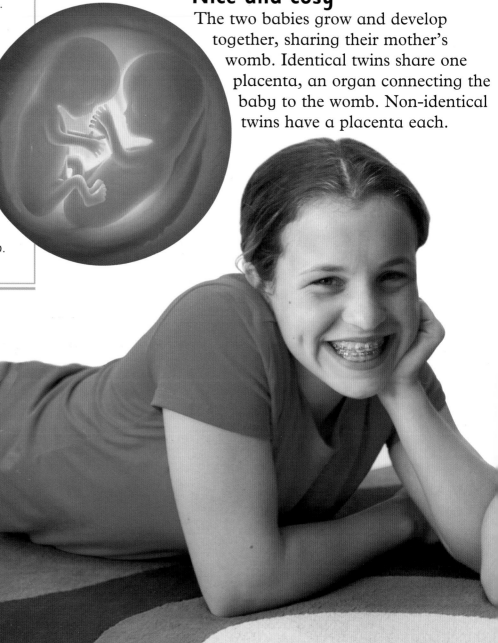

Nice and cosy

The two babies grow and develop together, sharing their mother's womb. Identical twins share one placenta, an organ connecting the baby to the womb. Non-identical twins have a placenta each.

Growing up

Identical twins often notice amazing similarities in their taste and behaviour. Sometimes they can even tell what the other is thinking!

Do identical twins have exactly the same fingerprints?

Multiple births

Even rarer than being a twin is being a triplet, or even a quadruplet.

 Triplets are rare. One in 8,100 natural pregnancies produces triplets.

 Quadruplets are rarer. One in 729,000 pregnancies produces quads.

 Having **quintuplets** or five children is usually a result of fertility treatment.

 There are currently only around 30 sets of **sextuplets** in the world.

Twins in the family

Once a couple has had one set of twins, they are more likely to have another. Also, if your mother, or her mother, is a non-identical twin, you may inherit the trait and have twins yourself!

Mirror twins

Some identical twins are called mirror twins. Often, one will be left-handed and the other right-handed, and their fingerprints appear to mirror each other.

Seven children are called "septuplets". All these children are non-identical.

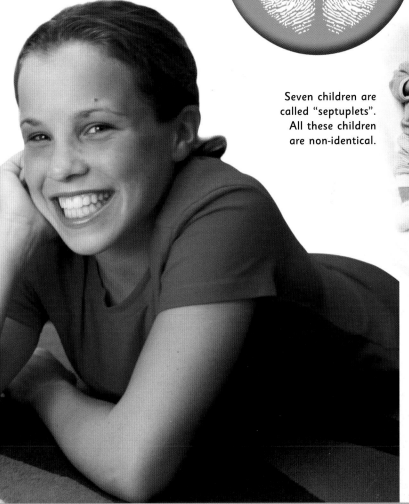

Record breakers!

Very rarely, septuplets or even octuplets (8) are born. The septuplets shown here are named Kenneth, Brandon, Nathan, Joel, Alexis, Natalie, and Kelsey. They were born in Iowa in America in 1997.

No, because the soft skin on their fingertips was moulded differently in the womb.

The early years

Babies' bodies grow very fast, but their brains develop quickly too. Learning to move around and talk are both huge tasks.

New skills

Children's brains are changing all the time as they learn new skills at an amazing rate.

 Most babies start to **smile** at around 6 weeks old.

 Babies learn to **drink** from a lidded cup between 6 and 12 months.

 Most babies can **feed** themselves from a bowl at around 15 months.

 Children can **name colours** by three years old.

 Five-year-olds can **brush** their teeth without help.

Big head

Babies have enormous heads in relation to the size of their bodies! As you get older, the rest of your body catches up.

Babies' big heads hold big brains! They need them because there's lots to learn.

Your body grows very fast during your first year...

Babies are so bendy, they can suck their own toes!

Four days

Newborns spend most of their time asleep. Even when they're awake they don't open their eyes much.

Six weeks

Babies cry when they are cold or hungry. By this age, they start to make cooing sounds too.

Six months

Babies have a lot more control over their bodies now. Their muscles are stronger, and they can sit up without help.

Being able to talk makes it easier to play with other children.

Chatterbox

By one year, a baby is trying to speak. By two, children can use 100 different words, and by three most know more than 1,000 different words.

... and hardly slows down during your second!

By three, children know the difference between boys and girls.

Two years

Children this age can walk and run, climb stairs, and kick balls. They are starting to get dressed alone but can't do up buttons, zips, buckles, and shoelaces.

One year

By this age babies can understand simple words. They also take their first few steps.

Growing up

As a child, you learn to walk and talk, run and jump, go to the toilet alone, eat with cutlery, read and write, and even make friends!

Making friends

By five years old, children can form friendships and play together. They start to care about what other people think of them.

What can you do?

Do you realize how much work goes into learning all these amazing skills?

 At six years old, most children can **do up** their own shoelaces.

 At seven, many children can **ride** a two-wheeled bike.

 Some children learn to **read** at four, some at five, and some at six!

 You should **write** fairly clearly by the time you are seven.

As your baby fat melts away, your features become clearer.

You're learning new skills such as skipping.

Sitting still and thinking are skills too.

There's still plenty of time to play after school hours.

Age 4–5
By this age, a child can speak clearly in basic sentences, and knows many thousands of words.

Age 5–6
It's time to learn to read, write, do sums, and maybe even start playing a musical instrument.

Age 7–10
Boys and girls tend to like different things at this age. They have more friends of their own sex.

What makes you grow?

Hair is here!
During puberty, both boys and girls get more hair on their bodies. Boys also start to grow hair on their faces and may start to shave.

Times when you grow fast are called growth spurts.

During adolescence, your thoughts and feelings change as much as your body.

Age 11–13
Your body is about to start growing very fast again. Boys have their growth spurt a year or two later than girls.

What's next?
The time when you are more than a child but not quite grown up is called adolescence. Your body changes a lot. This is known as puberty.

103

Growth hormone, a chemical produced by your pituitary gland.

Growing older

Adults keep growing, but more slowly than children. When you get older, your body takes longer to repair itself and replace worn-out cells.

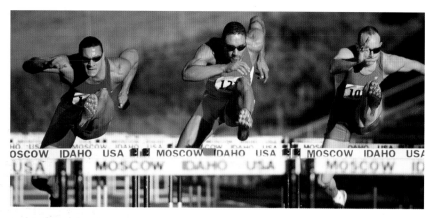

Life expectancy

Usually, the bigger a creature is, the longer it lives. Do you know how long humans live?

Butterflies have very short lives. Many live for only a month or two.

Cats kept as pets live longer than wild ones – up to 15 years.

People can live for 100 years. Women generally live longer than men.

The **largest tortoises** can live for 150 years. Some spend a quarter of their lives asleep.

Twenties

During your twenties you are at your peak. Your body has reached its adult size, so you don't spend most of your energy on growing.

Thirties

Because they're not growing any more, many people need to eat less so they don't get fat. Most bodies are strong and healthy, but athletes are already past their best.

Brittle bones

With old age, the bones and disks in the spine get weaker and thinner, so people get a little bit shorter.

A normal, healthy spine holds the body straight.

The spine starts to weaken.

Eventually, it forms an "s" curve and the head bends forwards.

What is the longest a person has ever lived?

Smile lines

With age, skin gets less stretchy and will not smooth out when you relax your face. This gives you wrinkles. Many cultures respect wrinkles as signs of wisdom and experience.

Silver surfer

Today people live longer than ever, thanks to advances in medicine. A healthy diet, exercise, and a young mind can make old age a happy time.

Old age

Papery skin, weak bones, stiff joints, and bad eyesight are common in old people. Most of the organs including the lungs and heart don't work as well as they used to.

Middle age

Organs and muscles are starting to get weaker. Skin on the face gets wrinkly, and hair starts to grey. Women stop having babies.

As you get older, your hair contains less melanin – the substance that gives it its colour.

Records prove that a French woman, Jeanne-Louise Calment, lived for 122 years.

What's in food?

People eat to get energy. You need a variety of foods to keep your body in peak working condition.

A balanced diet means eating everything your body needs.

Proteins
Meat, fish, eggs, beans, and nuts contain protein. Your body needs protein to repair its cells.

Carbohydrate
Bread, cereal, pasta, and sweet foods are mostly carbohydrates. You need them to give you energy.

Fat
Nuts and dairy foods, such as butter and cheese, contain fat. You only need small amounts of fat.

Takeaways and fizzy drinks are nice as a treat but no substitute for a good meal.

Eat your greens
Fresh fruit and vegetables are crammed with vitamins and minerals. Your body needs these to stay healthy.

Junk food
Fast foods like hamburgers and chips contain unhealthy amounts of fat and salt, and few vitamins.

What is a vegetarian?

Water

Your body is two-thirds water, but you're losing water all the time. You could live for several weeks without food but only for about three days without water.

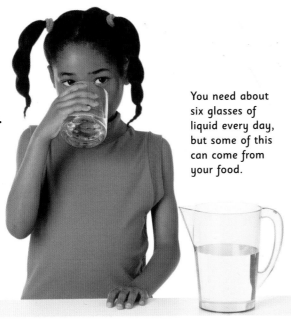

You need about six glasses of liquid every day, but some of this can come from your food.

Allergies

If your body reacts badly to a certain food and makes you ill, you may be allergic to it.

Wheat isn't good for some people. They cannot eat normal bread.

Nuts can be dangerous – even in tiny quantities – if you have a nut allergy.

Cows' milk doesn't suit some people, but they can drink sheep or goats' milk.

Sunshine food

You need vitamin D for strong bones. It is found in fish and eggs, but your body can produce it when sunlight falls on your skin.

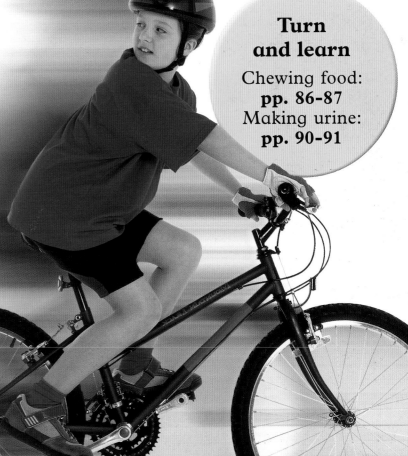

Turn and learn

Chewing food:
pp. 86-87
Making urine:
pp. 90-91

Fuel for your body

An orange gives you enough energy to cycle for 5 minutes. A chocolate bar gives you enough energy to cycle for 45 minutes.

Food gives you energy. The amount of energy you get from food is measured in calories.

A person who does not eat meat.

Sleep

When you sleep, your body rests. Your brain stops dealing with things in the outside world, and uses this time to sort out the events of the day.

Adults need about seven hours sleep.

A three-year-old needs about 12 hours of sleep.

A newborn baby can sleep for 20 hours a day. By six months, 15 hours is usually enough.

How much sleep?
As we grow older we need less sleep. Young adults need about eight hours, while those who are over 60 years of age may need only six.

Sleep patterns
Throughout the night, you move in and out of shallow and deep sleep several times. As the hours pass, sleep gradually becomes lighter until you wake up.

Awake

The yellow dots show...

Shallow sleep

Time for bed.

9   10   11   12   1

Deep sleep

108

What is insomnia?

Dreaming

Everyone dreams. When you dream, your eyelids flicker. This is called rapid eye movement, or REM, sleep.

Everyone dreams, but not everyone remembers their dreams.

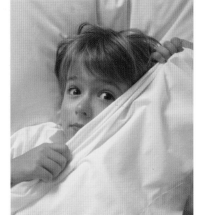

Nightmares

Nightmares are scary dreams that can wake you up and make you feel frightened or sad. During nightmares, people often think they are being chased or bullied.

What dreams mean

People are fascinated by what dreams mean. Some think that...

 ... **flying** can mean that you feel powerful and free of problems.

 ... **climbing up** can mean that you are struggling with something in your life.

 ... **falling** may mean you feel out of control or are scared of losing something.

... when you dream.

3   4   5   6

Good morning!

Sleep walking

During deep sleep, parts of the brain stay awake. People may talk, or get up and walk around. They usually don't remember they have done this.

The medical name for being unable to fall or stay asleep.

Doctors and dentists

When you are ill, you visit the doctor. First, the doctor examine you. Next, the doctor prescribes treatment or medicine to make you better.

The examination
The doctor asks you about your symptoms and then looks at and listens to different parts of your body.

Say "ah"
The doctor uses a stick to hold your tongue down and look at your tonsils. If your tonsils often get infected, you may need an operation to remove them.

Ears, nose, and throat
Doctors use an otoscope to examine your ears, nose, and throat. Swelling or itchiness may mean you have an infection.

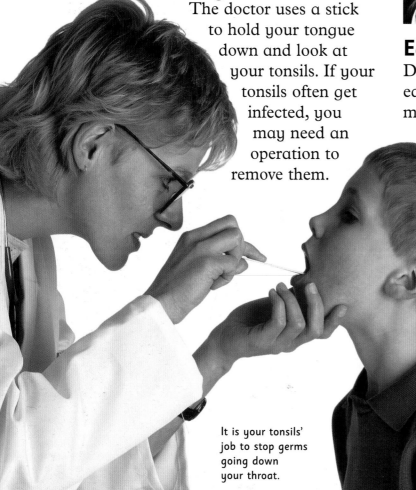

It is your tonsils' job to stop germs going down your throat.

Hear, hear
Doctors use an instrument called a stethoscope to listen to your heartbeat or to hear how well your lungs are working.

What is a paediatrician?

Tools of the trade

Doctors have a few simple instruments to help them examine their patients.

A stethoscope allows the doctor to listen to your heart or your breathing.

A rubber hammer is tapped against your knee to test your reflexes.

An ophthalmoscope has a bright light for looking at the back of your eyes.

Syringes are used to give people injections to stop them getting some diseases.

Medicine comes from a pharmacy. The doctor just gives you a prescription.

Eye spy

Opticians test your sight and work out whether you need glasses. They test each eye separately because often you can see better with one eye than the other. Your eyesight changes, so you need to get your eyes tested every year.

These funny-looking glasses help the optician find out exactly how well your eyes work.

Open wide

You can look after your teeth by brushing them, but you should still get them checked twice a year by a dentist. Hopefully, you won't need any fillings.

Brace yourself

Orthodontists are dentists who straighten out crooked teeth. They do this by fitting your mouth with braces to push your teeth gradually into the right position.

A doctor who specializes in children's illnesses.

Body language

You don't just talk with words – you also use your hands, face, and body. The look on your face and the way you stand can say a lot about how you really feel.

Personal space

People show how well they know each other by how close they stand or how often they touch. It's rude to stand too close to a stranger but normal to stand close to a best friend.

Only best friends and family can enter the **close intimate zone**.

The **intimate zone** is where people who know you well can stand while talking to you.

The **personal zone** is for people who know you but aren't close, such as teachers.

The **social zone** is where strangers stand while talking to you.

These girls are copying each other's body language.

Copying

Good friends often mimic each other's body language without realizing. They might walk in step, sit or stand in the same position, or copy each other's hand movements.

Who's in charge?

One of the things people signal with their body is whether they're in charge or somebody else is in charge. Leaning forwards or looking relaxed are ways of appearing to be in charge.

This boy's relaxed posture shows he feels very confident.

How does a dog show it knows you're in charge?

Learning gestures

You pick up a lot of your body language from the people you grow up with. Your gestures and the way you sit, stand, and walk are probably similar to your friends and family.

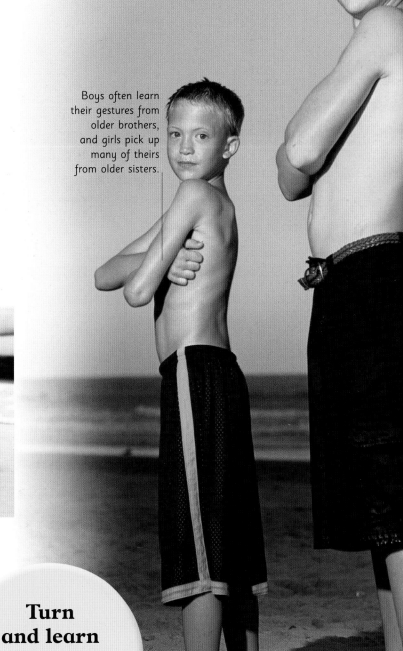

Boys often learn their gestures from older brothers, and girls pick up many of theirs from older sisters.

Open or closed?

When someone feels relaxed or friendly, they have an "open" posture, with arms and legs apart. If someone is nervous or awkward, they have a "closed" posture, with arms and legs close to the body.

Talking to animals

Animals can't understand speech but they often understand our body language. Dogs can sense who's in charge from body language. They need to be treated strictly or will start to misbehave.

Turn and learn

Muscles and movement: pp. 26-27

113

It lowers its body and tail and flattens its ears.

Use your hands

Most people move their hands as they speak, but what do their gestures mean? Some hand gestures mean the same thing all over the world, but others vary from place to place.

Speak to the hands
Hands seem to have minds of their own. When people talk, their hands move all over the place, even when they're on the phone!

Thumbs up

A raised thumb means "good" or "well done!" in North America. In Germany it means "one", in Japan it means "five", and in the Middle East and Africa it's impolite.

Making a circle
A finger touching a thumb means "OK" in North America, "worthless" in France, and "I want my change in coins" in Japan. In Turkey it can be rude.

Palms together

This is a sign of prayer in Christian countries, but in India it is used as a greeting. Indians place their hands together, make a slight bow, and say *"namaste"*.

Shaking hands
Shaking hands is a common greeting in many countries, but there are slight differences. A firm handshake is a sign of sincerity in Europe but is thought to be aggressive in Asia.

In some countries, women never shake hands with men.

In Sicily, this gesture, combined with a karate chopping movement, means "I hate you so much".

How does a diver say "shark" underwater?

Making a point

Pointing is one of the first hand gestures that people learn, and it means the same thing all over the world. Babies ask for things by pointing at them before they learn to speak.

Pointing with an outstretched arm means something is far away.

Turn and learn

The bones in your hands: **pp. 20-21**

Two fingers on the palm means the letter "n".

These 26 signs stand for the letters of the alphabet in British sign language.

Sign language

As they can't hear sounds, deaf people communicate by reading lips, using facial expressions, or using sign language. Sign language varies a lot from country to country.

Talking underwater

People can't speak underwater. Divers use a kind of sign language to communicate. It includes signs to indicate marine animals, such as turtles.

OK is shown by a finger touching a thumb, making a circle.

Stay at this depth is shown by waving a flat hand from side to side.

Stop is shown by a clenched fist and a bent arm.

115

Express yourself

Your face helps you communicate by showing how you feel. All over the world, people use the same facial expressions to show the six main emotions.

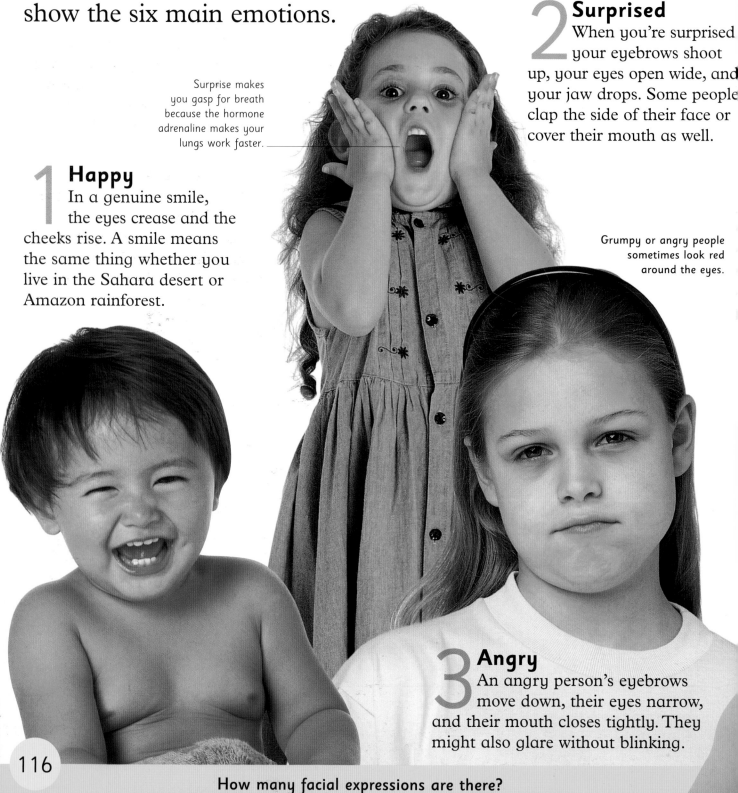

Surprise makes you gasp for breath because the hormone adrenaline makes your lungs work faster.

1 Happy
In a genuine smile, the eyes crease and the cheeks rise. A smile means the same thing whether you live in the Sahara desert or Amazon rainforest.

2 Surprised
When you're surprised your eyebrows shoot up, your eyes open wide, and your jaw drops. Some people clap the side of their face or cover their mouth as well.

Grumpy or angry people sometimes look red around the eyes.

3 Angry
An angry person's eyebrows move down, their eyes narrow, and their mouth closes tightly. They might also glare without blinking.

How many facial expressions are there?

Baby face
Babies communicate with their faces before they learn to talk. They smile, frown, and show all the main emotions.

Babies learn to mirror their parents' smiles from a very early age.

Turn and learn
How babies develop:
pp. 100–101

5 Afraid
Fear raises the eyelids, making the eyes look white. The mouth opens wide in horror, and blood may drain from the face, making the skin pale.

4 Sad
In an unhappy face, the mouth droops, the inner ends of the eyebrows go up, and wrinkles appear above the nose. Powerful feelings of sadness also make people cry.

6 Disgusted
Wrinkles across the nose and narrow eyes are signs of disgust. The sight of disgust in someone's face can make you feel disgusted too.

About 7,000.

Amazing facts about YOU

Skeleton and bones

Without a skeleton to hold you up, you'd collapse on the ground like a heap of jelly.

Your smallest bone is the stapes in your ear, which is smaller than a rice grain.

Weight for weight, bones are stronger than steel or concrete.

A baby has more than 300 bones but adults have only 206.

Muscles and movement

Muscles move your body by pulling bones. You use hundreds of them when you walk.

Every hair in your body has a tiny muscle that can pull it upright.

Your strongest muscle is the masseter (jaw muscle), which closes your mouth.

You use more muscles when you frown than when you smile.

Brain and nerves

Your brain is the body's control centre. Signals zoom to and from the brain along your nerves.

Nerves carry signals at up to 400 kph (250 mph).

Your brain is made of about 100 billion tiny cells called neurons.

The left side of your brain controls the right side of your body and vice versa.

The human eye can see a candle flame at night from 1.6 km (1 mile) away.

When you're bored, the pupils in your eyes get smaller.

Heart and blood

Your heart pumps blood around your body. It works nonstop without getting tired.

Your smallest blood vessels are ten times thinner than a hair.

Your body contains enough blood vessels to circle the world twice.

Breathing

Lungs take air into your body so that life-giving oxygen can enter your blood.

Laid out, the inside of your lungs is a third as big as a tennis court.

The fastest recorded sneeze reached 167 kph (104 mph).

In one day, you breathe in enough air to fill 33,000 drink cans.

Skin, nails and hair

The tough, protective surface of your body is almost entirely dead.

Every four years, you shed your own body weight in dead skin.

You have about 5 million hairs, but only 100,000 are on your head.

The thickest skin on your body is on the soles of your feet.

Fighting disease

Germs are always trying to get inside you, but your body fights back.

The dangerous lassa fever kills about a fifth of its victims.

Bacteria are so small that 1,000 could fit on the head of a pin.

The world's most common disease is the common cold.

Cancer happens when your own cells multiply out of control.

When you recover from an infectious disease, your body usually becomes immune to it.

Digestive system

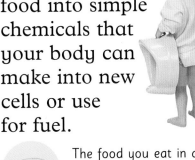

Digestion turns food into simple chemicals that your body can make into new cells or use for fuel.

The food you eat in a year weighs as much as a car.

You make enough spit in your lifetime to fill two swimming pools.

Your digestive glands start working as soon as you smell or see food.

Your tongue senses five tastes: salty, sweet, sour, bitter, and umami.

The smell of poo comes from a chemical called skatole.

Urinary system

Urine gets rid of chemicals that your body doesn't need.

You will make enough urine in your lifetime to fill 500 baths.

Asparagus can turn your urine green. Blackberries can turn it red.

Reproduction

The reproductive organs create new people from tiny specks of matter.

The most babies born to one mother is 69. Most were twins, triplets, or quads.

The first quintuplets known to have survived infancy were born in 1934.

Growth

As you grow, you slowly change into an adult, but it takes a long time!

The fastest-growing part of a baby's body is its head.

A girl is about three-quarters of her adult height at 7 years old.

A boy is about three-quarters of his adult height at 9 years old.

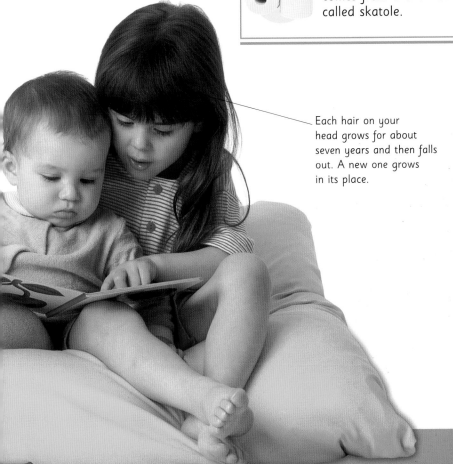

Each hair on your head grows for about seven years and then falls out. A new one grows in its place.

Through the ages

The human body is so amazingly complicated that it's taken doctors at least 4,000 years to figure out how it works. Their discoveries have led to many new ways of curing illness.

460–377 BCE
The Greek doctor Hippocrates is sometimes called the father of medicine. He was one of the first people to realize that diseases have natural causes and cures.

Before the time of Hippocrates, many people thought that diseases were punishments sent by the gods.

Medical firsts
Medicine has seen many inventions and discoveries over time.

250 BCE Egyptian doctors cut open corpses to find out how the body works.

100 BCE Chinese doctors discover that blood travels around the body in cycles.

1290 Spectacles are worn for the first time in Venice, Italy.

1500 A Swiss pig farmer performs the first Caesarian section on a living person.

1596 The Italian scientist Galileo Galilei invents the thermometer.

1684 Dutch microscopist Antony van Leeuwenhoek discovers blood cells.

1770 The world's first comfortable false teeth are used in France.

1796 English surgeon Edward Jenner discovers how to make vaccines.

1816 The stethoscope is used for the first time.

1818 James Blundell carries out the first blood transfusion.

What life-saving antibiotic did Alexander Fleming discover?

1852 Doctors use bandages soaked in plaster to make casts.

1853 Scottish doctor Alexander Wood invents the syringe.

1895 Wilhelm Röntgen accidentally discovers how to take X-rays of bones.

1928 An English scientist discovers antibiotics – drugs that kill bacteria.

1953 Scientists work out the structure of DNA, the chemical that carries genes.

1955 Doctors start using ultrasound scanners to see babies inside the womb.

1967 Surgeon Christiaan Barnard carries out the first heart transplant.

1971 Brain scanners come into use, allowing doctors to study living brains.

1978 Louise Joy Brown, the first test-tube baby, is born in England.

1985 Alec Jeffreys develops DNA fingerprinting.

2001 The first telesurgery (remote surgery) was performed by doctors in New York on a pateint in Germany.

2010 The world's first all-robotic surgery was performed in Canada.

The Italian scientist Lazzaro Spallanzani ate his own sick over and over to find out how the stomach works.

Modern medicine

Doctors know more about how the body works than ever before, but there are still some mysteries, like why we hiccup or how the brain works.

True or false?

Can you work out which of these facts are real, and which ones are completely made up?

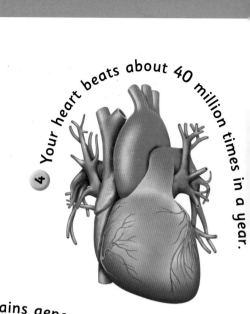

4 Your heart beats about 40 million times in a year.

3 Your DNA contains genes that come from your parents.

1 Coffee is bitter in taste.

2 The skill of riding a bike is stored in short-term memory.

122

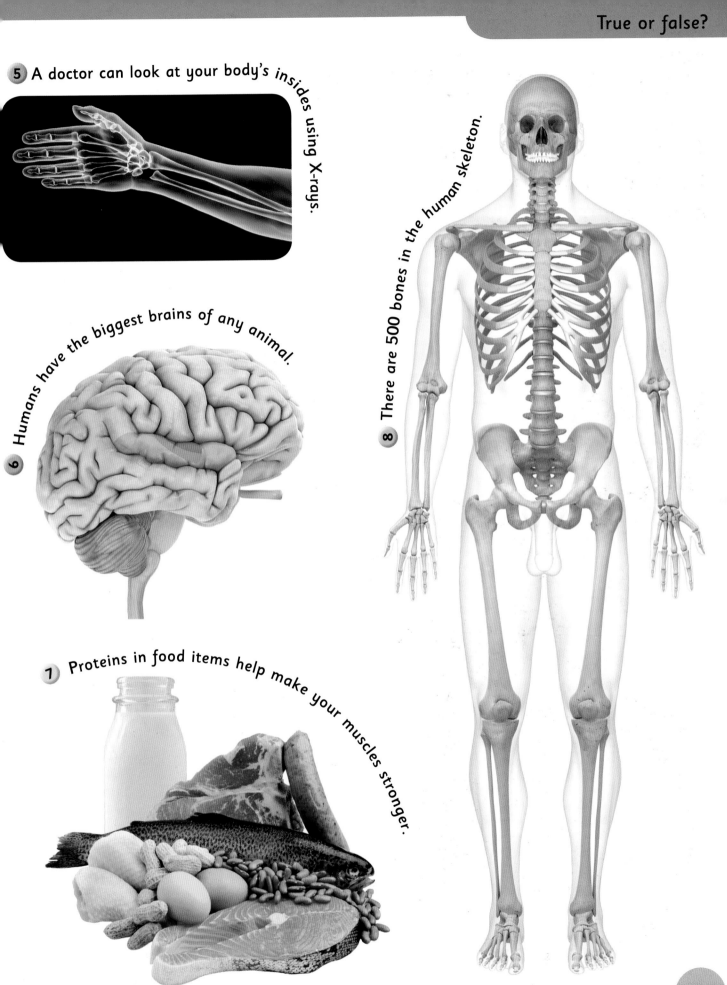

5 A doctor can look at your body's insides using X-rays.

6 Humans have the biggest brains of any animal.

7 Proteins in food items help make your muscles stronger.

8 There are 500 bones in the human skeleton.

123

Quiz

Test your knowledge
with these quiz questions.

4 What do the tiny hairs in your nose get clogged with if you have a cold?

A: Umami   B: Mucus

C: Marrow   D: Glucagon

5 People's hair turns white when they lose...

A: Acid   B: Melanin

C: Blood   D: Marrow

1 Which system uses powerful chemicals to control your mood?

A: Immune system   B: Hormone system

C: Digestive system   D: Urinary system

2 What do dust mites feed on?

A: Pieces of nails   B: Hair

C: Dead skin flakes   D: Bacteria

3 The sugar in sweets sticks to your teeth to form...

A: Enamel   B: Enzymes

C: Sodium   D: Plaque

6 Which vitamin can your body produce when you get sunlight on your skin?

A: Vitamin A   B: Vitamin B

C: Vitamin C   D: Vitamin D

7 Which bone is there at the very bottom of your spine?

A: Tail bone   B: Pelvis

C: Rib   D: Shin bone

8 What element gives the red blood cells their colour?

A: Potassium   **B: Phosphorous**

C: Carbon   **D: Iron**

9 When full, an adult's bladder can stretch to the size of a...

A: Plum   **B: Grapefruit**

C: Orange   **D: Melon**

10 Which of these muscles straightens your arms?

A: Tendons   **B: Biceps**

C: Triceps   **D: Pectoralis**

11 During the day, trees take in this gas from the air.

A: Carbon dioxide   **B: Oxygen**

C: Nitrogen   **D: Hydrogen**

12 The small flap of cartilage that shuts off your windpipe when you swallow is known as the...

A: Adam's apple   **B: Ligament**

C: Epiglottis   **D: Tonsil**

13 A cell's control centre is called...

A: DNA   **B: Nucleus**

C: Genes   **D: Cytoplasm**

14 Which chemicals stick to germs, telling other cells to attack?

A: Antibodies   **B: Urea**

C: Lysozyme   **D: Oestrogen**

15 The amount of energy you get from food is measured in...

A: Pints   **B: Centimetres**

C: Calories   **D: Kilograms**

16 In which country does a raised thumb mean "one"?

A: France   **B: USA**

C: Germany   **D: Japan**

Answers. 1:B 2:C 3:D 4:B 5:B 6:D 7:A 8:D 9:C 10:C 11:A 12:C 13:B 14:A 15:C 16:C

What am I?

Can you work out what is being talked about from each clue?

Thigh bone

Uterus

2: I am the biggest and strongest bone in your body.

Shoulder bone

Heart

1: I am a body part inside which a fertilized egg will grow into a baby.

Bladder

Ophthalmoscope

Stomach

Stethoscope

126

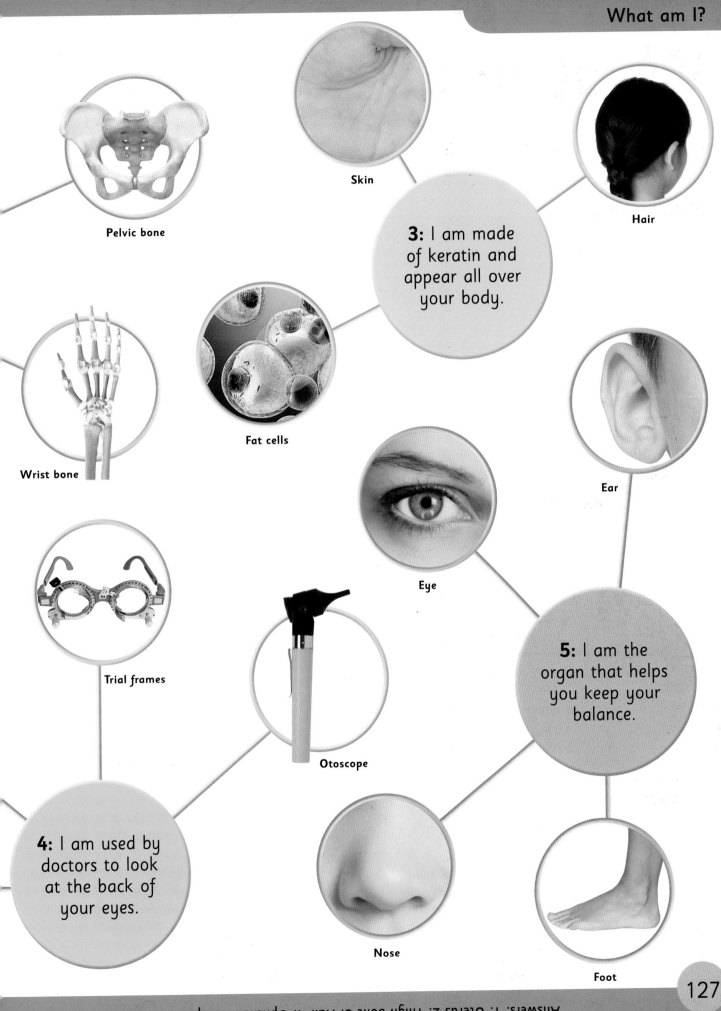

Pelvic bone

Skin

3: I am made of keratin and appear all over your body.

Hair

Wrist bone

Fat cells

Ear

Eye

Trial frames

Otoscope

5: I am the organ that helps you keep your balance.

4: I am used by doctors to look at the back of your eyes.

Nose

Foot

Answers: 1: Uterus 2: Thigh bone 3: Hair 4: Ophthalmoscope 5: Ear

Kidneys

Teeth

Stomach

Lungs

Sartorius

Tibialis

Where in the body?

Can you tell what each of these body parts is by matching the descriptions with the pictures?

2: This bony shell fits together like a jigsaw around your brain.

4: These are made of enamel, the hardest substance in your body.

6: When this is empty, its stretchy wall is full of folds.

1: These bumps on your tongue contain taste buds.

3: Blood picks up oxygen from these and carries it around the rest of the body.

5: This is a long tube where your food gets digested after it leaves your stomach.

7: Kidneys 8: Sartorius 9: Tibialis 10: Sole 11: Nail

Papillae

Skull

Nail

Sole

Intestine

8: This is the longest muscle in the body and helps you to squat.

11: These grow from a root under your cuticles.

7: These organs clean your blood and keep the water level in your body balanced.

9: This muscle helps bend your foot.

10: This is where the thickest skin of your body is.

Glossary

artery Blood vessel that carries blood away from your heart to the rest of your body

bacteria Tiny one-cell creatures found all around us. Some are helpful, others cause diseases

blood vessel Any tube that carries blood through your body

capillary Smallest type of blood vessel. Your body contains thousands of miles of capillaries

cell Smallest living unit of your body

diaphragm Strong, flat sheet of muscle under your lungs. You use it when you breathe

digestion Process that breaks down food into tiny pieces that your body can absorb and use

enzyme Substance that speeds up a particular chemical reaction in the body. Digestive enzymes speed up the breakdown of food molecules

epiglottis Trapdoor-like tag of skin that stops food going into your breathing tubes when you swallow

oesophagus Tube from your mouth that takes food to your stomach when you swallow.

genes Instructions that control the way your body develops and works. Genes pass from parents to their children

germs Tiny living things that can get into your body and cause illness. Bacteria and viruses are germs

gland Group of specialized cells that make and release a particular substance such as a hormone or enzyme.

hormone Chemical produced by one part of the body in order to change the way a different part of the body works. Hormones are made in glands and carried by the blood

joint Connection between two bones

mucus Slippery liquid on the inside of your nose, throat, and intestines

nerves Threads of tissue that carry high-speed signals around the body

nutrients Basic chemicals that make up food. Your body uses nutrients for growth and repair

organ Group of tissues that form a body part designed for a specific job. Your stomach is an organ

oxygen One of the gases in the air. You need to breathe in oxygen to live

proteins Vital nutrients that help your body build new cells. Food such as meat, eggs, fish, and cheese are rich in proteins

receptor Type of nerve cell that detects a change outside or inside the body, helping to create one of the senses. Touch receptors in the skin, for example, help create the sense of touch

reflex Reaction that is out of your control, like breathing or blinking when something gets near your eyes

saliva Liquid in your mouth. Saliva helps you taste, swallow, and digest food

system Group of organs that work together. Your mouth, stomach, and intestines make up your digestive system

tissue Group of cells that look and act the same. Muscle is a type of tissue

umbilical cord Tube joining a baby to its mother's body while it is still inside her

urine Waste liquid that passes out of you when you go to the toilet. Urine is made of water and chemicals your body doesn't need

vaccination Substance that is swallowed or injected to protect your body from disease

vein Blood vessel that carries blood towards your heart

vertebra One of the bones that link together to form your backbone, or spine

X-rays Invisible rays that pass through objects. X-ray photographs show the inside of your body

Index

Picture credits

The publisher would like to thank the following for their kind permission to reproduce their images:

(Key: a-above; c-centre; b-below; l-left; r-right; t-top)

1 Zygote Media Group 4 Corbis: Larry Williams (c); Science Photo Library: (bc); Getty Images: Barbara Peacock (cl). 5 Alamy Images: Aflo Foto Agency (tc), Janine Wiedel Photolibrary (cra), Pictor (cr); Corbis: Reuters (cla); Science Photo Library: (tr), Dr. Gopal Murti (crb), VVG (br). 6 Corbis: Laura Doss. 7 Alamy Images: Goodshoot (tr), Janine Wiedel Photolibrary (tc); Corbis: Jose Luis Pelaez (bl); 8 Science Photo Library: Dr. Gopal Murti (br), Martin Dohrn (cra). 9 Science Photo Library: (jar 3); Andrew Syred (tr), Prof. Aaron Polliack (jar 2), VVG (cl), (jar 1), (jar 4). 10 Alamy Images: RubberBall Productions (r); Corbis: Thom Lang (cl brain) Science Photo Library: J.L. Martra, Publiphoto Diffusion (bl); Victor de Schwanberg (cl heart), (cl kidney). 11 Alamy Images: Ablestock (bl), Comstock Images (button 5); Pictor (t), RubberBall Productions (c), (button 2). 13 DK Images: Oxford University Museum (ca); Science Photo Library: Pascal Goetgheluck (bl). 14 Science Photo Library: Sovereign ISM (bl). 15 Science Photo Library: D. Roberts (bl), Michael Donne, University of Manchester (br). 18 Science Photo Library: Andrew Syred (br), CNRI (cr), VVG (bl). 19 Alamy Images: Medical-on-line (cla); Science Photo Library: (cr), Department of Clinical Radiology, Salisbury District Hospital (tc), VVG (crb). 20 Alamy Images: Superstock (b); Science Photo Library: VVG (cr). 20-21 Science Photo Library: (t). 23 Science Photo Library: Mehua Kulyk (cl); Getty Images: David Roth (crb). 24 Science Photo Library: Astrid & Hans-Frieder Michler (cla), Prof. P. Motta/Dept. of Anatomy/ University "La Sapienza" (bl), Victor de Schwanberg (clb), VVG (cl). 25 Corbis: Kevin R. Morris (r). 26 Corbis: (l). 27 Corbis: Tom & Dee Ann McCarthy (clb). 28 Corbis: Ed Bock (tr), Thierry Orban/Sygma (cl); 28-29 Getty Images: Mike Timo. 29 Science Photo Library: Keith, Custom Medical Stock Photo (tl). 30 Getty Images: BodyOnline (c). 31 Corbis: Bryan F. Peterson (crb), Warren Morgan (bl); Colour Vision Store: (crbb); Science Photo Library: Dr. Goran Bredberg (crb), Mehau Kulyk (cra), Nancy Kedersha (tr), Omikron (cr). 32 Corbis: Jim Craigmyle (cl); Science Photo Library: Nancy Kedersha (br). 33 Corbis: Christine Osborne (tr); Science Photo Library: Michael Donne (tl). 34-35 Corbis: Norbert Schaefer (c), 35 Science Photo Library: Joe Bator (cb). 36 ImageState/Pictor: StockImage (cl); Science Photo Library: Omikron (br). 37 Science Photo Library: CNRI (br); Getty Images: Ross Whitaker (tl). 38 Science Photo Library: Gusto (bl). 40 Corbis: Lee White (background). 41 Alamy Images: BananaStock (br); 41 Corbis: Lee White (ca), (c); Colour Vision Store: (tr); 41 Science Photo Library: David Becker (cl). 42 DK Images: Natural History Museum (button 5); Science Photo Library: Mehau Kulyk (l). 44 Getty Images: Ross Whitaker (br). 46 Corbis: Tom Stewart. 47 Corbis: Dave G. Houser (tr), Firefly Productions (cb); Science Photo Library: Dr. Goran Bredberg (bc). 49 Science Photo Library: Susumu Nishinaga (tc). 51 Science Photo Library: CNRI (crb), Dr. P. Marazzi (br), NIBSC (cra), (cr). 52 Science Photo Library: Susumu Nishinaga (br), VVG (cr). 53 Science Photo Library:

NIBSC (cl). 54 Science Photo Library: BSPI, Gilles (bl), Professors P.M. Motta & S. Correr (tl); Roger Harris (cb). 54-55 Science Photo Library: Dr. Yogas Nikas (b). 55 Science Photo Library: (tl), NIBSC (tr), Roger Harris (c). 56 Corbis: Tom Stewart (bl); Science Photo Library: CNRI (cr). 57 Alamy Images: Shout (button 1); Photolibrary.com: Leanne Temme (cl); Science Photo Library: Alex Bartel (button 2), Astrid & Hanns-Frieder Michler (button 3), Martin Dohrn (tl). 58 Getty Images: Erin Patrice O'Brien (b). 63 Corbis: Stephen Frink (cr); Science Photo Library: David M. Martin M.D. (cla), Mark Thomas (tl), Matt Meadows, Peter Arnold Inc. (br), Proff. Motta, Correr & Nottola/ University "La Sapienza", Rome (crb). 64 Science Photo Library: Hank Morgan (cra). 65 Bubbles: Ian West (cl); Corbis: Don Mason (tl), Paul A. Souders (br). Getty Images: Stephanie Rausser (ca). 66 Science Photo Library: Damien Lovegrove (l), Matt Meadows, Peter Arnold Inc. (tr), Proff. Motta, Correr & Nottola/ University "La Sapienza", Rome (cr). 68 Alamy Images: Phoebe Dunn (cra); Science Photo Library: Andrew Syred (crb), (br); VVG (c). 69 Alamy Images: Pixland (tl). ImageState/Pictor: (bl). 70 Science Photo Library: VVG (bc). 71 Science Photo Library: Andrew Syred (ca); Lauren Shear (bc); Getty Images: Daniel J. Cox (tr). 72 Science Photo Library: VVG (ca). 73 Science Photo Library: Alex Bartel (tr), Martin Dohrn (c), VVG (br), (background). 74 DK Images: AMNH (tr blue), (tr green); Science Photo Library: Dr. Jeremy Burgess (br); Getty Images: Suzanne ann Nick Geary (bl). 75 DK Images: AMNH (button 1); Photolibrary.com: OSF (tr); Science Photo Library: Dr. Kari Lounatamaa (cla), Eye of Science (br), John Hadfield (cb). 76 Science Photo Library: Biophoto Associates (cl), Custom Medical Stock Photo (tc), Prof P.Motta/Dept ofAnatomy/ University, "La Sapienza", Rome (br). 77 Science Photo Library: CNRI (bc), Professoers P.M. Motta, K.R. Porter & P.M. Andrews (ca). 78 DK Images: AMNH (tr); Science Photo Library: Biology Media (br). 79 Science Photo Library: BSIP Estiot (tr); Getty Images: Chris Harvey (cl), Steven Peters (tl). 80 Corbis: Paul A. Souders (cl); Science Photo Library: Andrew Syred (button 4), Dr. Jeremy Burgess (button 1), K.H. Kjeldsen (b). 81 Corbis: Lester V. Bergman (cla); Getty Image: Digital Vision (br); Science Photo Library: Dr. Jeremy Burgess(tr), Dr. P. Marazzi (cr), Mark Clarke (bc). 83 Science Photo Library: BSIP, Cavallini James (crb), David M. Martin M.D. (br) Gusto Productions (cra), VVG (cr). 84 Corbis: Michael Keller (car); Powerstock: age fotostock (tl); Science Photo Library: Gusto Productions (tr). 85 Science Photo Library: Hattie Young (tl). 86 Science Photo Library: Dr. P. Marazzi

(bl), Tek Image (tl), VVG (c). 87 Science Photo Library: David. M. Martin M.D. (c); Zefa Visual Media: Chad Johnston/Masterfile (l). 88 Science Photo Library: David M. Martin M.D. (c) Eye of Science (cl). 89 Science Photo Library: David M. Martin M.D. (cr). 92 Science Photo Library: (c), (cr), BSIP, Cavallini James (tr). 93 Alamy Images: Robert Harding (c). 94 Robert Harding Picture Library: (c). Science Photo Library: Christian Darkin (tr). 95 Science Photo Library: Dr. Yorgos Nikas (tl), (tc), (tr). 96 Penny Arlon: (ca); Mother & Baby Picture Library: Ian Hooton (tr); Photolibrary.com: OSF (br); Science Photo Library: Dr. G. Moscoso (bl), Edelmann (bc). 97 Alamy Images: BM2 (tl); Photolibrary.com: OSF (tr); Getty Images: Ross Whitaker (bc). 98 Getty Images: (c). 98-99 Alamy Images: Big Cheese Photo (b). 99 Alamy Images: Robert Llewellyn (tr); Corbis: Brooks Kraft (br). 101 Corbis: Strauss/ Curtis (tl). 102 Corbis: O'Brien Productions (cl). 103 Corbis: Larry Williams (r); Rex Features: Phanie Agency/PHN (tl). 104 Corbis: Pete Saloutos cl. 104-105 Science Photo Library: Alfred Pasieka bl; Blustone (b). 105 Corbis: Roy Morsch (tr); Getty Images: Yann Layma (tl). 107 Corbis: Norbert Schaefer (cl). 109 Science Photo Library: Oscar Burnell (br); Zefa Visual Media: Robert Karpa/Masterfile (tc). 110 ImageState/Pictor: (tl), (cr). 111 Science Photo Library: Adam Hart-Davis (tc), Michael Donne (br), Pascal Goetgheluck (clb). 113 Corbis: Ariel Skelley (cl); Getty Images: Erin Patrice O'Brien (r). 114 Getty Images: Ian Sanderson (tr). 117 Corbis: Mark Tuschman (c); Getty Images: Tim Flach (tl). 118 Science Photo Library: Astrid & Hanns-Frieder Michler (button 1). 119 DK Images: Judith Miller/Elms Letsers (button 1); Science Photo Library: Dr. Tony Brain (button 2). 120 DK Images: British Museum (button 1), Judith Miller/TW conroy (button 9). 121 Corbis: Larry Williams (button 4), Michael Pole (r); Science Photo Library: (button 4), Edelmann (button 7), Victor de Schwanberg (button 8); Dreamstime.com: Robert Byron (clb) (button 11); Luchschen (bl) (button 12). 122 Dreamstime.com: Andrew Buckin / Ka_ru (tr). 123 Alamy Images: D. Hurst (bl). Fotolia: dimdimich (tl). 127 Alamy Images: Image Source (c). Dreamstime.com: Bentaboe (cl); Spectral-design (ca). 129 Dreamstime.com: Maryna Melnyk (clb) 133 Alamy Images: RubberBall Productions. 134-135 Alamy Images: Aflo Foto Agency. 136 Dreamstime.com: Monika Wisniewska (bc).

All other images © Dorling Kindersley
For further information see:
www.dkimages.com

Acknowledgements

Dorling Kindersley would like to thank: Elinor Greenwood, Lorrie Mack, and Fleur Star for editorial assistance, Dorian Spencer Davies for additional illustration, Mary Sandberg for additional design assistance, Julia Harris-Voss for picture research, and Chris Bernstein for compiling the index.